121. I La Chanson de Guillaume *and* La Prise d'Orange

Critical Guides to French Texts

EDITED BY ROGER LITTLE, WOLFGANG VAN EMDEN, DAVID WILLIAMS

La Chanson de Guillaume

and

La Prise d'Orange

by **Philip E. Bennett**

Reader in French
University of Edinburgh

Grant & Cutler Ltd
2000

© Grant & Cutler Ltd
2000
ISBN 0 7293 0420 5

DEPÓSITO LEGAL: V. 4.645 - 2000

Printed in Spain by
Artes Gráficas Soler, S.A., Valencia
for
GRANT & CUTLER LTD
55–57, GREAT MARLBOROUGH STREET, LONDON W1V 2AY

Contents

To the Memory of Jeanne Wathelet-Willem

Preface

The following study forms part of a double project, the other part of which is an edition and translation of the *Chanson de Guillaume* (*4* in the continuously numbered bibliography at the end of this volume), which will be the reference edition of the *Chanson de Guillaume* in this Guide. It will be studied together with *La Prise d'Orange*, for which the reference edition will be Claude Régnier's synoptic edition (*5*). Although both poems may be said loosely to belong to the epic cycle of Garin de Monglane, tracing the biography of that hero and his clan over several generations, only the latter is strictly a cyclic poem.

The study within one volume of these two major twelfth-century epic texts poses severe problems, mostly of scope and scale, but has the advantage of permitting a particularly rich perspective on the material contained in the poems and on the evolution of the poetics of the epic at a crucial stage in literary development in France. The links between the works are close at all levels. Apart from the mere unifying presence of Guillaume, the essential hero of the poetic cycle known by his name, we find in the heroi-comic treatment accorded him in both *chansons* the seeds of an ambivalent attitude to heroes in general which will be a mark of the evolving romance and, later, of European narrative fiction in general. Indeed the evolution of the poems through three of the most creative generations in the history of French literature provides a paradigm of rapidly changing forms and ideologies. Neither text is totally free of lyric or romance features, whether in their surface realisations or deeper within their poetic structures. Both, however, remain distinctly epic, belonging incontestably to the genre of the *chansons de geste*.

The study consists of four chapters. The first, introductory, considers the nature of the objects being studied; the second and third (Chapters 1 and 2) deal with some of the major problems posed by the individual poems; the final chapter tackles problems common to both songs, and approaches them systematically from an intertextual point of view. Clearly such a study cannot but be based on the century or more of intense scholarship which has now gone into the study of the *chansons de geste*. Exhaustive citation would be intolerable, and my debt to these illustrious academic forebears is hereby generally acknowledged. Citations will, of course be made where germane to particular arguments.

Initially I wish to thank the British Academy and the University of Edinburgh for financial support of work done towards this volume. My especial thanks are due to Professor Wolfgang van Emden, who first suggested the study many years ago, and whose patience and encouragement, like that of Mr Raymond Howard of Grant & Cutler Ltd, has been invaluable. Professor van Emden's highly scholarly and illuminating comments on my first draft have been most helpful. Versions of some of the chapters have been read at meetings of the Société Internationale Rencesvals, the Denys Hay Seminar (University of Edinburgh) and the Scottish Medieval Group. To all my colleagues whose thoughtful criticisms have helped me clarify my views I offer my gratitude. The blemishes are all my own.

Edinburgh

Introduction

The Object of Study

There are certain problems common to the study of all medieval texts which are not found, or not usually found, in the study of more recent texts. The most fundamental of these, and that which is most frequently overlooked by literary critics, particularly of the modern schools, is the definition of the object of study. At least since the nineteenth century we have been used to dealing with texts whose material presentation (strophe or chapter and paragraph divisions, layout on the page including orthography, capitalisation and punctuation) as well as content have been closely controlled by the author, and are the product either of the author's express intention or of close consultation between the author and the publisher. With the exception of the works of a few authors from the end of the Middle Ages, like Christine de Pizan, Guillaume de Machaut, Jean Froissart and Charles d'Orléans, no such confidence can be placed in the text as the perpetuation of an author's specific design when we approach medieval literature.

This is partly due to the material conditions of the transmission of texts by copying longhand from a previous copy to produce a new manuscript, or by recitation or singing (whether or not this involved reading from a manuscript either before or during the performance). Such methods of transmission inevitably led to a high incidence of accidental variation. More significant, however, is the attitude of the people of the time to literature in general, which was to be glossed (with incorporated commentaries), adapted and improved. Part of the process of adaptation resulted from the absence of the notion of a standard language, which, coupled with the rapid evolution of French and English in particular, meant that texts were constantly being rewritten in the current dialect of the scribe or his patron. Most pertinently though, all literature was in the public domain, so that, even if 'writers' such as Turold, Marie de France or Chrétien de Troyes 'signed' their works, scribes and continuators felt free to 'improve' them.

This applied to some extent even to sacred texts and to the works of Ancient 'authorities', into which the commentaries of teachers became incorporated owing to the pedagogic system of glossing, until they attained the status of the 'changeless' text itself. With vernacular romance, an essentially written genre which proclaimed its links to the learned Classical tradition, we nevertheless find greater instability in the text than in authoritative works of the Classical or Biblical traditions, an instability which becomes extreme in the essentially oral genres of lyric and epic poetry which had no tangible links to the canon of ancient writing. This mutability of the text, which has been seen as a condition of the existence of medieval literature (*136*, pp.70–75; cf. *61*), has a drastic effect on the study of the *chansons de geste*.

The Old French epic is affected by the process in two ways. Firstly, although it is inevitably known to us only in versions transcribed into manuscripts, and therefore has the air of being of the same kind as vernacular romance or learned or sacred literature in Latin, up to, and perhaps into the twelfth century, it was firmly rooted in the oral tradition. The study of epic traditions alive in the twentieth century has shown that although singers claim to reproduce their received material faithfully they effectively reinvent their song with every singing, embroidering freely on the minimal storyline, which alone is essential to the tradition, using inherited formulaic expressions and motifs or themes (templates of broader textual segments and episodes) to generate their poem not from memory but by an active process of recomposition (*95*, pp.13–29). This close relationship to traditional, oral forms may to some extent account not only for the omission (or insertion), inversion and conflation of whole episodes and characters in the story of a *chanson de geste* but also be responsible for the many variations of detail found in the texts. Although to a great extent the manuscript

versions of epic resemble those of romances, and textual copying
and revision account for many simple variants (*123*, pp.684–86), the
greatly increased number of variants found in epic texts may not be
unrelated to the formulaic, oral origins of the genre. That poems
also existed as a constellation of traditions is shown by the number
of claims preserved in the written texts to the current poet's
knowing the 'true' version, and belittling the 'ignorance' of his
competitors, as in *La Prise d'Orange* (*PO*), *AB*,[1] ll.18–19 (cf. *10*,
ll.1265–70). However, the Old French epic in its manuscript
versions does not behave in the same way as genuinely oral modern
epics, which are rarely susceptible to being reduced to a single
coherent version: they can frequently be represented if not by one
then at least by a small number of closely related 'originals' with
other versions derived from them by means well-known from the
study of romances and learned literature (*68*, pp.405–07; *123*,
pp.664–66). Moreover, as we can see from Beroul's *Tristran*,
Wace's *Roman de Rou* or Jordan Fantosme's *Chronicle*, writers
firmly in the learned tradition were quite capable of composing in
an 'oral' way, for a variety of reasons only a few of which we can
deduce today (*55*, pp.325–29).

    Wherever we lay the stress in our approach to the study of
chansons de geste, on their oral antecedents or on the written
versions surviving in the manuscripts, we are faced with the same
fundamental problem, that of the absence of a single unified object
of study. Even when there is only one witness to a song, as in the
case of *La Chanson de Guillaume* (*ChG*), we cannot escape the
internal testimony of the text's mutations or the presence of a
multiplex tradition supporting the poem which we find in
comparisons with related texts, notably *PO* itself, *La Chevalerie
Vivien* and *Aliscans*. The case of a poem such as *PO*, which exists in
three different recensions preserved in a total of nine manuscripts,
merely makes this state of affairs more obvious.

---

[1]These letters refer to groups or 'families' of manuscripts conserving
'redactions' (medieval editions) of the poem. *PO* exists in three such
'redactions' today, conventionally known as *AB*, *C(E)* and *D*.

This alarming lack of consistency in the texts as objects of study is, however, frequently camouflaged from the modern reader by the production of critical editions, which, by comparing different manuscript versions aim to reproduce the 'original' poem, or at least that lost version held to have been the source of all extant manuscript versions. Based on theories developed at the end of the nineteenth and beginning of the twentieth century, which treated medieval vernacular writers as if they had the same artistic views and aspirations as a modern author, or as a Classical Greek or Roman one, this approach to producing texts often involved inventing readings to produce self-consistency in the text when the manuscripts failed to produce a 'convincing' answer. The method, originally applied to romances and similar texts for which an individual author could be posited, held sway in epic studies as well until, in the 1950s, the Neo-traditionalists — so called because they renewed the theories of the nineteenth-century Traditionalist (or Romantic) school, which considered epic the authorless creation of the 'people' — removed the author from his consecrated place (*70*; *95*; *103*; *115*). Since then editors have adopted a variety of strategies for editing *chansons de geste*. Along with the continued habit of producing critical editions, aimed now at reproducing as closely as possible the text of one manuscript chosen as the best representative of the tradition, it has become habitual to produce synoptic editions, presenting sequentially or in parallel, either all the manuscripts of a tradition or, more frequently for practical reasons, a representative, critically chosen selection. Such an approach allows the modern student of the texts to take as object of study something which at least approximates to the protean complexity of the medieval tradition.

The two poems studied in this volume provide an interesting example of this problem in all its complexity. One, *ChG*, cannot be studied in isolation as a discrete object despite its existence in only one manuscript. Full account must be taken not only of the surrounding narrative and poetic traditions relating to Guillaume but also of the internal evolution through time of the tradition (possibly represented by individual authors) as it generates the extant text. With the other, *PO*, we have, along with evolution over time, to take account of what appears to modern students as 'mutability in space', since the tradition presents us with a number of simultaneously surviving written texts offering more or less closely related parallel versions.

La Prise d'Orange: Mutability and the Manuscript Tradition

PO comes to us as a cyclic poem. That is, whatever its origins as an independent song in the early twelfth century, it exists today only as part of the organised poetic biography of Guillaume d'Orange and his extensive family, which was established towards the end of that century. As with a number of other songs dealing with Guillaume and his clan which had led a separate existence, *PO* was clearly altered to take account of aspects of the legend which postdate the first allusion we have to the existence of our poem ca 1122, and to allow it to fit reasonably smoothly into the chronological continuum created by the cyclic manuscripts.

It is in this cyclic form that the Guillaume poems achieved their true popularity, so that in the thirteenth century commercial scriptoria produced copies for wealthy aristocratic or bourgeois patrons. For reasons no longer totally clear to us each house produced its own version, so that what survive are three 'editions', or redactions. Although, as Claude Régnier has shown in his synoptic edition (*5*, pp.16–28), it is possible to trace all these versions back to a cyclic archetype, they represent such divergent approaches to the transmission of the poem that it is impossible to re-create that archetype in a critical edition. However, Régnier considered *AB* the 'vulgate' (most representative) version, and issued an edition of that version independently (*6*), although as his stemma shows (*5*, p.28) there are more intermediaries between the archetype and *AB* than between it and either *C(E)* or *D*. Distinct differences can, moreover, be observed between the two branches of *AB*. The four manuscripts making up the *A* branch have perhaps the greatest number of epic features: the most rigid and lyrical *laisse* structure, the greatest use of *laisses similaires* and formulaic

repetition. They also show the greatest number of those other
features (illogicalities and incongruities of plot, and discordancies of
vocabulary and style) which have led many critics to suppose that
the cyclic *PO* is essentially a parodic text (*6*, pp.30–31; *90*). The two
B manuscripts, prepared much later than *A* and representing the
most extensive elaboration of the whole cycle, while very close to *A*,
consistently smooth out by small retouches those features which
have led the poem to be considered either inept or comic, according
to the critic's own sensibilities. This version thus produces a slightly
dull, but more conventional *chanson de geste*, albeit one still
strongly marked by features borrowed from either romance or
courtly lyric. Redaction *C(E)* takes this process even further,
although both its manuscripts are earlier by perhaps half a century
than *B*'s. The very epic form of the poem, its tight *laisse* structure
and formulaic patterning, is adapted to the newer ideals of narrative
structuring typical of romance, while fewer incongruities of plot are
evident and the vocabulary is more banal. The most remarkable
redaction in many ways, however, is *D*. This version is so disjointed
and garbled, while relying very heavily on formulaic composition,
that it may be held to be a very poor and arthritic example of epic.
Opinions differ sharply as to whether *D* was produced from a very
defective written copy, or by a *jongleur* improvising from a very
defective memory (*113*; *101*). A third interpretation, squaring the
circle, is that *D* stands as proof of an assertion long put forward by
proponents of the idea that all surviving epic poems were produced
by scribes taking down a text at dictation from a *jongleur*. Since
there is an intrinsic link between the rhythms of the chant and the
text produced by a 'singer of tales', so that, once forced to break his
rhythm to accommodate the slower pace of the transcriber, the
singer quickly loses his grip on his song and his art, it may be that
D's poor version was produced by just that method.

One way in which the *D* version can be shown to be
significant despite its weaknesses lies in the fact that it derives
directly from the cyclic archetype and not, like *AB* and *C(E)*, from
one of the lost intermediaries between the archetype and the
surviving manuscript groupings. Thus it helps us see the ways in

which the other redactions have coped with problems raised by disruptions in the tradition. One small example of this concerns the message which Arragon, the pagan commander in Orange, sent to Tiebaut, the absent ruler of the town, requesting help. In *D* this is in its natural place after the second capture of Guillaume and Orable by Arragon's men (*laisse* 46, corresponding to *laisse* 53 of *AB*, and *laisse* 57 of *C(E)*). In the other versions, owing to an error in a common ancestor, this message is sent after the first capture of the lovers (*AB laisse* 42, *C(E) laisse* 44), and they then try to gloss over the error by different means in the correct place. In *AB* when an adviser suggests that Arragon sends the message, he replies 'Mes le message ai ge ja envoié' (l.1536), while in *C(E)* he replies 'Ce voel jou otroier' (l.1729), thus generating an illogical duplicate message. In fact we see at work two different strategies for dealing with a textual problem in an age when 'cut and paste' was not an option. *AB* treats the adviser as ill-informed, and assumes literary awareness in the audience; *C(E)* assumes that an audience receiving the text aurally, even if read from a manuscript, will either not remember, or not care, that the message has not only already been sent but has been depicted as being received by Tiebaut in a detail unknown to the other versions. Other comparisons of this sort enable us to see the shifting relationships between the various extant redactions and the archetype, without allowing any possibility of re-creating that archetype. Nor indeed would such a re-creation now be desirable, since so many of the changes in the extant versions are the result not of unintentional error but of conscious decisions by those responsible for producing them.

It was an awareness that *PO* was not one poem but a small galaxy of related texts that led Claude Régnier to publish his multiple edition. Unfortunately he later complicated the issue by extracting from it, for less advanced students and a general readership, an edition of *AB* alone. He chose *AB* as being 'la plus proche de l'original, la moins marquée dialectalement' (*6*, p.5), although both parts of this statement are contentious: the latter takes a twentieth-century view that *francien* (the dialect of the Ile-de-France) is the standard, from which others are deviations; the former, as we have seen, is not totally defensible from Régnier's own *stemma*. To complicate matters further his edition is based on the 'best manuscript' principle, so that effectively for most modern readers not only redaction *AB* but the whole poem (and thus subconsciously the archetype) is represented by one thirteenth-century manuscript of the *A* family. Yet this manuscript is not only the product of a long process of copying and revising by a number of hands, but also derives from a poetic tradition already well over half a century old when the cyclic archetype was composed.

That tradition had begun with a song, referred to in the *Vita* of St William of Gellone (one of the supposed historical prototypes of Guillaume d'Orange), in which the capture of the town was a simple military expedition to dislodge Muslim 'pirates' who had invaded the Rhone valley. This story was repeatedly revised to take account of other poems dealing with Guillaume and his clan, so that by 1150 at the latest Orable was introduced as the heroine of *PO*, identified with Guibourc (Guillaume's wife in *ChG*) and presented as a Saracen princess previously married to Tiebaut (one of Guillaume's traditional adversaries). Later revisions reduced the brutality of the earlier texts, increasing the atmosphere of *courtoisie* in the poem, before the current, possibly parodic, version appeared between 1190 and 1200 (*52*, pp.2–7; *5*, pp.89–90), and generating the extant cyclic texts in the course of the thirteenth and fourteenth centuries.

La Chanson de Guillaume: Mutability in Time

At first blush the fact that *ChG* exists in only one manuscript and never became part of the great cyclic developments of the later twelfth century would suggest that the problems related to it would be less complex than those of *PO*. That, however, is far from the case, and in many respects it is even harder to determine what is the object of study when dealing with *ChG* than when dealing with *PO*. The nub of the problem lies this time in the history of the elaboration of the surviving text, and in the relationship of certain elements of that text to other poems found in the compilations of the Cycle de Monglane.

The relationship of *ChG* to the cyclic texts is highly complex. Material relating to the first episode of the poem (the defeat and death of Vivien) is re-elaborated within the cycle in *La Chevalerie Vivien*, in which Vivien's death is the product of his own brutal *hubris* (*18, S*, ll.91–135; cf. *72*, 1, pp.279–82), as he has sole command of the army from the start and provokes the Saracen invasion, which is a simple act of aggression in *ChG*. The cowardly braggarts, Tedbalt and Estourmi, who create the impasse leading to the massacre in *ChG*, are absent from the later poem and Vivien's thirst for martyrdom, seen in his exaggerated vow not to retreat one spear's length from an enemy he has sought out, is alone responsible for his death and that of his comrades. There is no evidence of an earlier version of *La Chevalerie Vivien* independent of *ChG*, so one would expect the influence to be in one direction. However, the presentation of Vivien is ambivalent at times in *ChG* and it is not impossible that, as the older text continued to evolve into the thirteenth century, it reacted to the newer image of Vivien given not only in *La Chevalerie Vivien* but also in *Les Enfances Vivien*, a poem of the early thirteenth century dealing with Vivien's childhood and early manhood. That *La Chevalerie Vivien* might be the isolated development is shown by allusions to Tedbalt in another late cyclic continuation of *Aliscans*, *Foucon de Candie* (*45*, p.20), and to Estourmi in *Les Enfances Vivien* (*45*, p.7).

A similar relationship exists between the last long episode of *ChG*, of which the giant Rainoart is the real hero, and the cyclic poem *Aliscans* (*72*, 1, pp.235–41). However, in this case it can be shown that both the last 1,500 or so lines of *ChG* and the whole of *Aliscans* were elaborated from a 'Chanson de Rainoart', which probably already existed ca 1150. This is not to say that in the lost poem Rainoart and Guillaume both figured in a plot identical to the one we find in the extant poems. The perception by poets in the later twelfth century that Guillaume, with his Rabelaisian laugh, Gargantuan appetite and habit of killing enemies with a blow of his mighty fist, and the rustic giant with his club were in some ways reflections of each other brought their 'biographies' into close harmony: each character's tale ends with a heroi-comic account of retirement to a monastery. It is likely therefore that they were brought together within the cycle. Distinct differences between the surviving versions make it hard to accept that either *ChG* or *Aliscans* is simply a 'crib' from the other, although reciprocal influence between the surviving poems is not to be ruled out as both continued to circulate in the first half of the thirteenth century.

The other main allusions to material related to the Guillaume Cycle all come within the speech by Vivien in which he finally sends his cousin Girard to fetch help from Guillaume. In it he attributes to himself a number of victories elsewhere assigned to his uncle. Notably he claims to have killed Tedbald l'Esturman (= Tiebaut) in a battle beneath the walls of Orange, which must refer to an earlier state of *PO*, and to have won the victory over Borel and his sons, which may reflect a battle involving Borel and a number of members of Guillaume's clan recounted in a now lost poem, preserved in the eleventh-century Latin 'Hague Fragment' (*72*, 1, pp.69–76). He equally takes credit for the victory in a battle where the Emperor Louis fled in panic, which is generally assumed to be drawn from an episode in *Le Couronnement de Louis* and alluded to also by Guillaume in *Le Charroi de Nîmes* (*24*, *AB*, ll.2264–90; *20*, ll.220–55).

This absorption by *ChG* of material originally extraneous to itself reveals a song evolving dynamically and reacting to changes in the epic world around it. A similar picture emerges from a consideration of the text itself and its history. Apart from the obvious break at line 1980, which has led many scholars to treat the poem as two entities usually called '*G1*' and '*G2*' respectively (*72*, 1, pp.144–48), introducing the Rainoart material and relocating Guillaume's headquarters from Barcelona (captured from the Moors by a Frankish army including Count William of Toulouse in AD 803) to Orange (in keeping with the cyclic epic tradition), we find two other episodes either artificially inserted (Girard-Guischard, ll.938–1302) or totally reworked on existing material (Gui, ll.1303–1980). Although the borders of these episodes are not sharply defined, and the reviser has woven them with some care into the existing fabric of the song, their autonomy is revealed by a number of narrative illogicalities and by inconsistencies in the treatment of characters. There is also a change in the treatment and use of the refrain, which, from being a timeless incantation in the first section (despite its apparently precise reference to 'lunsdi al vespre'), becomes in the second and third episodes a mere chronological signpost, signalling the length of a battle or explaining a character's hunger. Finally, they reveal a change of tone, particularly the 'Gui' episode, which corresponds to the original second panel of the traditional diptych of death and revenge, where comedy, and probable parody, come much to the fore. This same episode reveals one other surprising facet: a distinct change in prosody compared to other parts of the poem, which probably points to a complete reworking of the poem in Anglo-Norman England some time after 1150 (*54*, pp.269–77).

These conscious interventions in the poem by successive revisers are compounded by the inevitable changes made to the text by copyists. Although not all the changes attributed to scribes by Jeanne Wathelet-Willem (*131*, 1, pp.66–78) can now be accepted as such, it is clear that the widespread habit of glossing an existing text, adding explanations, particularly to clarify relationships between characters, did afflict at least one scribe through whose hands *ChG* passed, while others undoubtedly added to the Anglo-Norman complexion of the poem's language and prosody.

All these modifications and rearrangements mean that the version of *ChG* that we find in the London manuscript is akin to a cathedral, whose structure and décor has evolved through the centuries, but which continues to form an aesthetic whole, despite the disparate nature of its architectural elements. The stages by which the poem has been assembled are themselves the subject of some controversy. While the poem undoubtedly contains some very archaic material, I would argue that the apparent influence of the thought of St Bernard de Clairvaux on the Vivien section indicates that the earliest preserved stratum of text cannot predate the 1120s (see below pp.35–37). The dates around the middle of the twelfth century, or even into the second half of the century, at which the Girard-Guischard, Gui and Rainoart material was added to the poem's original fabric are even harder to determine. While François Suard suggests a date for compilation ca 1150 (*3*, p.xxv), Duncan McMillan opts for the early thirteenth century (*2*, 2, pp.115–31, esp. 116). Jeanne Wathelet-Willem, after an exhaustive review of the evidence, suggests that the poem as we have it (bar scribal interference) dates from around 1150. However, some evidence she cites would allow the Rainoart material to have been added as late as ca 1160 (although the allusion to 'Rainoart au tinel' in a poem by Giraut de Cabreira used to provide this dating appears to refer to *Aliscans* rather than *G2* and may be to the underlying 'Chanson de Rainoart'), and the Gui material (referred to by the troubadour Arnaut Daniel) as late as ca 1180 (*131*, 1, pp.651–55).

This unity in diversity has posed problems for both editors and critics. Some studies of the song ignore the illogicalities, discrepancies and contradictions which abound in the poem, particularly across the divide of ll.1980–81, and explore the poem as if it were in its current form a structural and ideological unity produced by one controlling sensibility (*3*, p.xx; *114*, pp.14–18). They also assume that a thirteenth-century audience (that receiving the poem as preserved in the British Library manuscript) would have accepted the text as a unified whole, a presupposition which we should not make in the light of Chrétien de Troyes's strictures on inept popular story-tellers and the need for *conjointure* in literature (*25*, ll.1–26).

The problem posed by the construction *ChG* is highlighted by the fates of characters called 'Girard', 'Guischard' and 'Gui/Guiot/Guiotun/Guielin'. Guischard and Guielin are captured by Saracens (ll.1721–22) together with Bertrand, who has not otherwise figured in the poem, and are released by Rainoart (ll.3006–156) in a pair of episodes found also in *Aliscans* (*7*, ll.293–322; 5578–904), which, like the corresponding episodes in *ChG*, cross the boundary of the defeat leading to the journey to Louis's court and the entry of Rainoart. In *Aliscans* Girard is also captured, and all these characters are clearly identified as nephews of Guillaume. From this we might deduce that the adaptation of the original *ChG* to the 'Chanson de Rainoart' began with the entry of Desramé (1.1707), and that the author of the Gui episode adapted his material to the rest of the song by having 'Guiot/Guiotun' captured at ll.2072–85, being content to have him released later under the name of 'Guielin'. Yet if we assume this order of construction the current ending of *G1*, which is totally at odds with *Aliscans*, becomes inexplicable. The alternative explanation is that the reviser responsible for melding *G1* and *G2* inserted the lines relative to the capture of Guillaume's nephews into *G1*, and that a later hand both inserted the episode of Guiot's capture (generating a pair of characters who were re-amalgamated by default at the release of 'Guielin') and altered ll.1721–22, removing Girard and having only Bertrand identified as Guillaume's nephew. Girard and Guischard, however, remain problematic, since two characters by those names (one Guillaume's nephew, one Guibourc's nephew) have been killed (ll.1134–1227) in an episode probably added by the same hand to which we owe the Gui episode. There is no attempt to camouflage the duplication of Guischard, but revisers and scribes took more care with the prominent Girard: suppressed from the list of captured at both ll.1722 and 3055–56, he is referred to by Alderufe (1.2100) as 'Girard quis cadele' (approximately 'Girard the Captain' — unless we are to see yet another synonymous character in this reference), and resurges at Guillaume's side among the other freed prisoners (1.3155) with the ungrammatical soubriquet 'fiz cadele' (which we might gloss 'Son of the Captain'), which most editors correct to 'quis cadele'. This causes new difficulties for our perception of how *ChG* was assembled, as the evidence seems conflicting. The best compromise explanation is probably that the *G2* redactor was aware of the 'Girard-Guischard-Gui' interpolations and tried to adapt to them, but failed to adjust the end of *G1* and missed the reappearance of Girard at the end of his own section, an omission which a later hand tried to rectify by creating a new 'Girard' unrelated to the young warrior of *G1*.

The consequence of all this is that editors find themselves confronted by a serious dilemma, and for the modern reader it is more true of *ChG* than of almost any other medieval text that the conception we have of it depends on the edition used. What should be the editor's approach? Should it be, like Duncan McMillan (*2*), to accept the manuscript 'warts and all', and, preserving the compound *laisses* with mixed assonances and respecting the highly irregular line lengths, intervene only to correct evident linguistic errors? Or should it be, like Jeanne Wathelet-Willem (*131*, 2, pp.730–1073), producing unified mono-assonanced *laisses* and regular decasyllabics even at the cost of considerable rewriting, to set out to re-create linguistically and prosodically the poem that might have existed as it came from the pen of a poet working on the borders of Normandy and the Ile-de-France in the mid-twelfth century? Should one go further and, like Hermann Suchier (*1*), edit only the first 1980 lines of the poem, on the grounds that the Rainoart material does not belong to the original song? None of these approaches can totally avoid criticism, but the 'archaeological' approach of Wathelet-Willem is the most fraught with danger, since it is possible that the Rainoart material was incorporated in the song in Anglo-Norman England (*49*, pp.86–89), and it is almost certain that it was there and not in Continental France that the extant 'Girard-Guischard-Gui' episodes were written (*54*). As with critical editions of multi-manuscript texts like *PO*, the attempt to reconstruct the lost original of *ChG* is likely to produce merely another new version of the text, one unknown to any medieval audience.

Conclusion

The question of defining what will be the objects of the following study is more complicated for the texts involved than even for many other texts of the Middle Ages, most of which nevertheless reveal similar layers of complexity. It is certainly harder to resolve than for any modern work of literature. What follows will, therefore, inevitably be based on a compromise. For *PO* it will concentrate on the *AB* redaction in Claude Régnier's edition, referring to other published redactions or unpublished manuscripts only where such references significantly alter our perception of the material being discussed. For *ChG* I shall refer to my own edition (*4*), whose principles of adherence to the text of the only surviving manuscript are close to those of McMillan's authoritative SATF text (*2*), while taking fully into account both the complexity of the 'literary artefact' contained in that manuscript and the importance of sidelights thrown by other songs from the Guillaume Cycle on to the problems raised.

1. La Chanson de Guillaume

New Heroes for Old

Like most epics the *chansons de geste* are structured so as to set off the qualities of one warrior against another and to pit him against a whole society. The opposition is not between values, since the warrior highlighted by the poem shares the essential aspirations of his society; if he finds himself isolated from it, it is because of the purity of purpose with which he espouses those values.

Unlike the heroes of courtly and Arthurian romance the hero of the *chanson de geste* does not have to leave the community in order to discover his own higher identity or fulfil his personal destiny even in exile or under ban of outlawry: Roland, Ogier de Danemark, Renaut de Montauban, Guillaume d'Orange and Vivien work out their fate surrounded by fellow warriors, even if the bright fire of their purpose leads them to momentary isolation at the crisis or culmination of their destiny. As a result, the notion that the epic hero is estranged from his society even when he is at the heart of it and striving to uphold what he sees as its ideals is similar to that propounded for modern literature of the hero as outsider (*133*).

The sense of community in the *chansons de geste* leads us to use the word 'hero' in two distinct ways, which are not mutually exclusive in the context of epic poetry. Firstly it can be used in the way common to the language of literary criticism to refer to the work's protagonist. This, however, is not always useful in dealing with a genre which does not in every case identify such a principal character. No manuscript of the *Chanson de Roland* names Charlemagne's nephew in a 'title' or *incipit*, and early criticism refers to the 'Roman de Roncevaux' (*92*, pp.6–8); an alternative and frequent title for *Renaut de Montauban* is *Les Quatre Fils Aymon*, which reinserts the central figure into a family and social group. Even in a poem such as *ChG*, which uses this formula to name the song and its hero at the end of the first *laisse* (*4*, l.11), problems can arise, since it is not clear from what follows that announcement that there is just one protagonist in the poem. In the *chanson de geste* as a manifestation of the epic genre the older meaning of a privileged being whose prowess and capacities as a warrior border on the supernatural, who shares something of the aura of the divine or who is at least in direct communication with the world of spiritual beings is the more pertinent. This can apply to Charlemagne or Roland in the *Roland*, to Huguelin and Gormont in *Gormont et Isembart* (*78*; *50*) and in different ways to Guillaume and Vivien.

The hero so designated achieves his destiny, which is not infrequently some form of self-immolation in the cause of his higher idealism, through a series of conflicts. These are usually of two types. Firstly there are the battles with a physical enemy, the Saracens in *ChG*, in which the hero's qualities are manifested directly. The role of the enemy is to provide a channel for the expression of the hero's capacity for bravery, suffering and loyalty while demonstrating that skill as a fighter which evokes admiration in a warrior society. Only rarely, such as at the opening of *PO*, where they refuse combat, do Saracens constitute an obstacle on the hero's path to self-fulfilment. That role belongs to other characters in the hero's own camp, who have something of the heroic stamp, but fail at a crucial moment. It might be a companion, such as Oliver counselling Roland or Bertrand advising Guillaume to summon reinforcements (in the *Roland* and *Le Couronnement de Louis* respectively), a pusillanimous king, usually called 'Louis', more concerned with his own position than with the wider cause of Christendom, or a commander whose nerve fails in the crisis, such as Tedbalt de Burges in *ChG*. Inevitably the 'obstacle' merely acts as a stimulus to the hero, enabling him to manifest his essential being by reacting against the pressures that would make him conform to the more reasonable (or more human) model proposed by the unheroic society that surrounds him.

In *ChG* there are indeed many heroes, in both senses evoked above, and whose status is tested in a variety of ways. Despite the announcement of line 11, Guillaume is far from being the most prominent hero in the existing version of the song. In the first 900 lines of the poem he merely provides a background for Vivien's heroism; later he is displaced, even replaced, by a second nephew, Gui, and by his brother-in-law, Rainoart, for whose very special place in the poem see pp.49ff. below.

Guillaume's role and status as hero in *ChG* is highly ambiguous. Like his pagan counterpart, Desramé, he is physically absent from the whole of the first battle, although entering earlier, at l.933, whereas Desramé appears in person only at l.1707, each of them taking on a vital moral force, all the more palpable because they remain 'unseen' powers. The main feature of the presentation of the 'Hook-Nosed Marquis' in the Vivien episode thus becomes his reputation, as a warrior, as an overlord and as a mentor. In all of these respects he is seen as at least equal to Louis, the emperor, whose position as suzerain should make him the guarantor of victory, saving the lives of his vassals by effective military and legal action (*122*, pp.46–47, 49–50). Louis has a much better reputation in *G1* than he does in the cyclic poems, but that is undercut even more severely than Guillaume's when he finally appears and refuses point blank to help his vassals (ll.2530–31).

The first mention of Guillaume in the text proper comes when Vivien responds to Count Tedbalt's request for counsel:

> 'n'obliez mie Willame al cur niés,
> sages hom est mult en bataille champel;
> il la set ben maintenir et garder.
> S'il vient, nus veintrums Deramed.'
>
> (55–58)

Here we have a complete sketch of Guillaume as the wise commander, the sound strategist and tactician who never fails in battle. This reputation is so firmly established that it gives rise to envy, voiced in the reply of Esturmi, Tedbalt's nephew:

'En ceste terre, al regne Lowys,
u que arivent paen u Arabit
si mandent Willame le marchis.
Si de tes homes i meines tu vint mil,
vienge Willame, et des suens n'i ait que cinc,
treis u quatre, que vienge a eschari,
tu te combates et venques Arabiz,
si dist hom ço, que dan Willame le fist.
Qui ques prenge, suens est tote voie le pris!
Cumbatum, sire, sis veintrum; jo te plevis.
Al pris Willame te poez faire tenir!'
(60–69)

Apart from establishing a clan unity dividing two sets of uncles and nephews (a vital, representative pairing in the epic — *87*, pp.72–73, 88–90), the speech instantly defines the Berrichons as anti-heroic against the Narbonnais. This it does by appealing to an ancient tradition in epic poetry, represented, for instance, in the scene in the Anglo-Saxon *Beowulf* in which the envious Unferth disputes Beowulf's heroic credentials before his combat with the evil giant Grendel (*9*, pp.66–67). The very attempt to undermine the hero's reputation is self-defeating, as here, because it reaffirms it in the very challenge. It also reveals a fundamental flaw in a society which takes warrior heroism as its benchmark, since antagonistic rivalry between individuals inhibits effective action against society's enemies. Nevertheless, despite being placed in the mouth of Esturmi, the lines do allow the poet to make an ironic comment on the concept of reputation itself, and indeed on the epic concept of the 'guarant': nothing permits us to suppose that Esturmi's assessment is wrong when he says that Guillaume's sole presence in a large army under another's command sees victory popularly attributed to him within the 'epic' community.

The speech is also notable for shifting back and forth between the general (ll.60–62 and 67) and the particular, in a way which deliberately sets Tedbalt up in opposition to Guillaume. Apart from giving us a measure of his reputation, and a mark to which his rivals for reputation can aspire, the lines explain the constant longing for Guillaume's physical presence which characterises the long agony of Vivien and his troop. This longing finds expression in a number of ways, which could lead us to dub this section of the poem 'Waiting for Guillaume'.

The motif of waiting is first introduced in lines marked by heavy sarcasm, in which Vivien recalls Tedbalt's drunken boasts of the previous night, and asserts that, now he is sober, wiser counsel will prevail (ll.120–22). It returns (l.485), also in Vivien's voice, immediately after his formal lament over Guillaume's absence (ll.480–81) and may be perceived in the self-delusion, by which Vivien mistakes Girart for Guillaume or Louis (l.453) when the young squire returns to the field shouting the imperial war cry 'Munjoie!' (l.440). Immediately before the final catastrophe this is transmuted into a desperate assertion made to reassure the survivors that Guillaume will come (ll.750–52). It is of signal importance that the poet identifies himself with his characters in the formulation of this motif by adding his own laments over the absence of Guillaume from the battlefield to theirs, and by associating it with the 'lunsdi al vespre' refrain on each occasion (ll.471–72; 487–88).

The complementary motif of actually sending for Guillaume is interwoven with these. It surfaces first in Tedbalt's unnerving question as to whether he had sent for the count or not (l.127), a question which is met by a short and untruthful response from Esturmi, who places all the responsibility for no message being sent to Guillaume firmly on his uncle (ll.129–30), conveniently forgetting his own contribution. The question is transformed into an assertion by Tedbalt that he will now send for Guillaume, and will not fight without him (ll.196–201); yet we cannot perceive that the count of Bourges has learned any real wisdom. Not only does he urge Vivien to take a cowardly, and futile action (to hide behind some rocks) while he 'sends' for Guillaume, but he impugns the latter's honour by adding 'qui combatera s'il ose' (l.199), which takes us back full circle to the rivalries of the previous night. The sequence, held in suspense through much of the first section of the poem, closes only with Vivien's ultimately sending Girart to bring Guillaume with the desired aid (ll.633–34). It is noteworthy also, the local commander (Tedbalt) and his *de facto* replacement (Vivien) having failed for different reasons in their role of 'guarant', that Vivien turns not to the emperor but to his uncle and mentor to fill that role (*122*, pp.47, 52).

Into both of these series, interrupting and extending them as well as encapsulating them and translating them to a higher plane, is inserted the series of prayers pronounced by Vivien, asking that God, or the Virgin Mary, send either Guillaume or Louis to him (ll.562–64; 797–98; 824–26; 894–96; 906). The second and third of these prayers are inserted into the 'Gethsemane' sequence, in which Vivien prays first to be spared and then repents of that weakness. The call for God to send Guillaume can therefore not be seen as a desire to be saved in any way. Nor does Vivien have the feudal and ecclesiastical insights of Turpin in the *Roland* (*17*, ll.1740–51) who vindicates sending for Charles by saying that the Emperor will both avenge the fallen and ensure their burial in consecrated ground. Such thoughts are far from the Vivien of *G1*, whose only concern is the defeat of the pagans. The prayers also equate Guillaume with the ultimate 'guarant', the emperor himself, a Louis quite the equal of his father and not yet debased by his portrayal in *Le Couronnement de Louis* and *Le Charroi de Nîmes*, or indeed in *G2*. As such, Guillaume is the model that Tedbalt and others can strive to emulate. However, Vivien, with uncharacteristic modesty for an epic hero, refuses to consider himself on a par with his uncle, at least when the question first arises (ll.86–88). Later, during the 'Gethsemane' scene, he asserts that his intrinsic prowess is equal to that of his uncle, but accepts that Guillaume's greater powers as a warrior and a commander come from longer experience (ll.828–34), a first sign in the poem that we are moving away from the universe of absolutes which characterises the epic, to one of relatives, more usually associated with the romance.

The cumulative effect of this drenching of the first part of the poem with appeals from characters and poet alike is to endow Guillaume with an unassailable moral authority and heroic power.

The reality, when he finally enters the scene, is somewhat different. The character as person seems more than a little distanced from his abstract reputation (*60*, p.266). We find him, in fact, in a moment of repose, comfortably reminiscing with his wife, Guibourc, over her conversion to Christianity and his good fortune in marrying her. The rosy glow of this domesticity is made all the more remarkable by its structural position within *G1*. On the one hand the fact that the pair have just left vespers provides a parallel with the opening of the poem, where Tedbalt and Esturmi were similarly leaving the evening office. Such thematic repetitions, themselves constituting a sort of refrain, are frequently used in *chansons de geste* to articulate the poems and assure their unity. Unlike the repeated allusion to the seven-year campaign of conquest in Spain in the *Roland* (*17*, ll.1–6; 703–05; 2609–11), or the messages which summon Guillaume from pleasanter pursuits to rescue France and Louis yet again in *Le Couronnement de Louis* (*24*, *AB* ll.1368–70; 1414–24; 2198–205; 2632–40), the effect here is not cumulative but contrastive, with the peace of Guillaume's palace set against the hurly-burly of Tedbalt's court. The contrast also extends to the two men, with Guillaume's sober piety used as a foil to Tedbalt's drunken irreverence.

    The impact of this interlude of domesticity is all the greater as it is set between two reports of battle. As in the opening scene, the portrait of the hero leaving vespers is the prelude to the arrival of a messenger with tidings of disaster. In both instances the audience is privy to the news before it is broken, so that the atmosphere in each castle can be assessed against an external reality. The revelry in Bourges and the domestic self-satisfaction in Barcelona are presented as equally misplaced in the context of the reality of grim struggle without. Indeed, the image of Guillaume's Barcelona as a paradise of unalloyed peace, which we might have been inclined to accept as a haven from the hellishly sterile land which Girard has to cross to reach it from l'Archamp, which is equally infernal, guaranteeing the identity of the hero with his reputation by its presentation of majesty (cf. *88*, pp.235–45, 357–442), has already been undermined by the poet at the moment at which we perceive it. Guillaume, we are told, has just returned from a battle in which he lost 'grant masse de ses homes' (l.936). Although we are not told whether this battle has ended in victory or defeat for Guillaume, the latter seems implied by the expression. In any case, like the Charlemagne of the closing lines of the *Roland*, Guillaume is exhausted by his continual efforts ('Et ensurquetut nel purreie endurrer: / fer et acer i purreit hom user', ll.1022–23) and reluctant, he says, to commit himself anew. Like his later casuistical distinction between running away and leaving the field (ll.1225–28), the poet's assertion that Guillaume is saying this only to test Guibourc is transparently disingenuous. We are witnessing a depreciation of the hero which will continue throughout the rest of the poem, notably in the 'Girard-Guischard' episode (ll.1027–1302) where the victory expected to occur in the second part of an epic on the theme of defeat and revenge is swept away from the hero in a matter of nine lines (1120–28), and which will be marked by the replacement of Guillaume by other heroes.

We have already witnessed this to some extent in the message which Vivien sends to Guillaume to summon him to l'Archamp (ll.635–78). In this message the young warrior inserts himself as hero and bringer of victory into a series of battles which the audience will have been conditioned by tradition to consider as Guillaume's triumphs (see above, p.18). The main beneficiaries of the demotion of Guillaume are Gui, in *G1*, and Rainoart in *G2*. Gui's intervention in the poem, announced by Vivien and then suspended, is dramatically effective, not only in his rising phoenix-like (a resurrected Vivien as the Saracens call him — ll.1853–54) from the 'ashes' of the great fireplace to which Guillaume would return him, but in his ability to represent both the trickster hero and the warrior hero (*60*, pp.267–70). He it is who single-handedly saves his uncle when he has been overwhelmed by pagans, and then delivers the *coup de grâce* to Desramé, whom Guillaume, out of a misplaced sense of chivalry, would spare. Gui's rebuttal of Guillaume's world view is brutal and earthy, and the older man immediately accepts his logic, so that although the battle is won Guillaume has been stripped of both his military reputation and his moral authority.

To a large extent that authority had been lost long before Guillaume's mantle fell on Gui, and transferred to Guibourc. Although she never leaves the castle it is she, more than Guillaume, who guides events to a successful conclusion as she assumes the role of a sort of universal Earth-Mother. She provides vast restorative feasts for Girard and Guillaume when they come 'home' crushed by defeat; with uncanny prescience she summons her own vassals (from where we are not told and cannot guess, since she is presented as foreign and of pagan origin) to replace the men lost by her husband for the second time in a matter of days; she lies to them to persuade them to go to l'Archamp to collect easy booty, and beguiles them with images of the women she will give them (again from her own unaccountable store of riches) as wives on their safe return. She it is also who arms Girard and Gui, as in *G2* she will defend the town with her women under arms, and provide Rainoart with the sword which allows the victory to be won at last (ll.3320–42).

If the provision of food may be seen as an archetypically feminine function, the raising of troops, arming of warriors and defence of castles belongs, at least in epic, to the masculine sphere. In this way Guibourc is not only a source of universal provision for the Christians, but, in the sense that Micheline de Combarieu du Grès (*64*, pp.55–77) defines it for *Aliscans*, the real source of their victory. This becomes abundantly clear at the start of *G2* when she puts the backbone back into Guillaume, tells him it is not yet time to retire to a monastery, and sends him to Laon to enlist the help of Louis (ll.2420–31). There he will find an emperor who is as much of a broken reed as himself. He will, however, find his own father, Aimeri, and the rest of the Narbonnais, and most importantly, Guibourc's brother, Rainoart. If it is he who strikes the winning blows at l'Archamp, replacing all other heroes, it is Guibourc who, at first unwittingly but later quite consciously, plays the role of intermediary allowing Rainoart to fill the void which has opened in Christian ranks.

This void is partly the product of Guillaume's great age (especially in *G2*), although elsewhere in the epic patriarchal antiquity is no bar to heroic activity, and even here Guillaume's own father shows no signs of loss of vigour. The essential point in *ChG* is that the hero's age is being used as a symbol of his belonging to the class of *seniores*, not just older men, but great feudatories and overlords. In this way Guillaume is constantly equated with Louis and, as with any king, his availability for heroic action is limited by the constraints of the royal function (*84*, esp. pp.113–20). As a result he is eclipsed by a series of younger heroes (Vivien, Girard, Gui and Rainoart) in a repetitive sequence. Unlike Louis, however, Guillaume never loses his authority completely, as we see at Laon; but, like Charlemagne, whose moral heir he is in much of the Guillaume Cycle (*127*), he continues to operate as a warrior king. Even so, at the end of *G1* he is demoted to the role of ostler, while his nephew, Gui, performs the action of dispatching the supreme commander of the pagans, a role which Charles was still permitted in the *Roland*, when he overcame Baligant.

This demotion and replacement of representatives of the older order actually starts very early in the poem. Tedbalt de Burges is introduced as a character exactly equivalent to Guillaume. He is a count, accompanied by his nephew, with the prestige of his position ('mult honuré / des meillurs homes de rivage de mer', ll.51–52; 169–70) and of whom Vivien says, even in the depths of his degradation, when he has fled and been symbolically stripped of his arms by Girard who 'knights' himself with them, that he is 'prodome' (l.464). Yet it is clear that he is a negative version of Guillaume, coming drunk from vespers (l.32), exposing himself to the enemy, and thus committing himself to battle (ll.203–04), contrary to Guillaume's instruction to Vivien to keep his helmet out of sight 'desi qu'al champ u fiere od le poig destre' (l.165). It is not, however, Tedbalt's attitude to scouting which ultimately condemns him, although it does precipitate his disgrace. It is rather the mixture of drunkenness and boasting which the poet of the Vivien episode scathingly castigates in his person.

It is a well-established feature of heroic poetry that in advance of an action the hero boasts formally, in an atmosphere of solemn ritual, of the deeds he will accomplish (*122*, pp.52–53, *53*, pp.480–82). Thus Beowulf pledges himself to fight Grendel (*9*, pp.70–71), the warriors of Brihtnoht's army have sworn to fight the Danes at Maldon (*36*, pp.35–38), and Roland boasts that he will not give up a single packhorse that has not been paid for in sword blows (*17*, ll.751–59), having previously boasted that if he dies in a foreign land it will be in a posture of conquest (*17*, ll.2860–67). As an ancient Germanic custom it is reported by Tacitus, who states that the Germans pledged themselves when drunk, and confirmed the pledge when sober (*35*, pp.119–20). In just this way Tedbalt ritualises his assertion that he will fight Desramé. He calls for wine (ll.89–90) and immediately pronounces the binding words

> 'Ainz demain prime requerrum Arrabiz;
> de set liwes en orrat l'em les criz,
> hanstes freindre et forz escuz croissir!'
> (91–93)

after which he solemnly drinks with Esturmi (l.95). However, unlike the earlier heroes, for whom this was a sacred rite, and even unlike Roland, in whose case the ceremony is lightly Christianised by being associated with one of the great Church feasts (*17*, l.2860), the meaning seems to have gone out of the ritual for Tedbalt. He was, after all, already the worse for drink, and whereas in all other cases the boasts lead to action, for him they lead only to a hangover, confusion, a pathetic attempt to live up to his words and a disgraceful panic-stricken flight, leaving Vivien and his men to be slaughtered.

In this way Tedbalt is further differentiated from Guillaume, and it is not Tedbalt alone, but a whole epic motif that is called in question, since Tedbalt's nephew is so closely implicated both in the boast and the débâcle which follows. Guillaume does indeed consume food and drink in large quantities between battles, either alone or in the company of Girard or of other warriors, but this never produces a formal boast. For these characters food and drink are both a restorative and symbolic of their prowess, but they are desacralised. Also, in fitting into the wider thematic of hunger and thirst which runs through the poem, the feasting of heroes, whose appetites, despite Guibourc's assertions, are not a mark of their true martial value (both Guillaume and Girard march out from their heroic banquets to defeat), is seen to be on a lower level than Vivien's hunger and thirst, which take on Christological overtones (*72*, 1, pp.190–97).

In this aspect of his character Vivien has frequently been equated with Roland, either as a copy or a revised version (*72*, 1, pp.185–86), or as a parody (see below, pp.100ff.). All of these interpretations impose on *ChG* a view of literature which is essentially modern, and, even if in part it can be made to fit the romance, is quite at odds with the epic's constant re-exploitation of traditional motifs (*98*, esp. Ch. X, 'Les paroles gelées'). In neither of its versions (*G1*, ll.760–928; *G2*, ll.1988–2052) should Vivien's death be read with reference to Roland. The latter's hieratic death in peaceful surroundings ministered to by angels reflects a view of the Crucifixion found in Carolingian and Romanesque sculpture, where death is a transcendental act of divine volition exempt from physical pain. In *G1* Vivien's hunger and thirst, his drinking from a polluted stream inducing vomiting (recalling the sponge soaked in vinegar of the Gospels), the wounds in his arms, hands and side, the sense of abandonment by all, even by God, and the implied references to the agony of Gethsemane in Vivien's prayers, all point to a later view, initiated in the writings of Bernard of Clairvaux and the Cistercians, which puts increasing emphasis on the suffering of Christ as a physical as well as a spiritual being, a development possibly inspired by a reaction to heresies like Catharism which denied the corporeality of Christ (*116*, pp.221–29). In this way Vivien, like Roland, is portrayed as a true martyr, his death being an imitation of Christ. The revision of *G2*, with its emphasis on communion and last rites, far from returning us to the atmosphere of the *Roland*, transforms Vivien into a confessor: a sort of Everyman model of Christian dying. What distinguishes him from Roland in both versions is not the absence of a hieratic distancing in the depiction of his death, but the same Christian asceticism which marks him out in the rest of the poem from Tedbalt, Esturmi and even Guillaume.

The *laisse* in which Tedbalt drinks and boasts ends with the bald line 'Et Vivien s'en alad a sun ostel dormir' (l.96), the simplicity of which is a blunt condemnation of all that goes on in Bourges. To refer to this asceticism as almost monastic is not out of place. If the *jongleur* still kits his hero out with the visual trappings of the heroic commander, Vivien's preference for a personal vow to God not to flee in the face of the enemy over a public boast to perform signal deeds of arms (ll.291–92; *122*, p.43), the keeping of which torments his conscience in his last moments (ll.807–12; 901–05), and which is transmuted into a mutual vow of support between himself and his men at the opening of the battle (ll.305–13), as well as his refusal of wine and drunkenness all associate him with the new military orders of the Hospital and the Temple, which arose in the early twelfth century as a period of desperate sacrificial consolidation in the Holy Land replaced the euphoria of the conquests of the First Crusade (*91*, pp.167–73). In their *Rules* and in theoretical writings such as Bernard of Clairvaux's *De Laude Novae Militiae* of 1128, dedication, obedience, refusal to flee the field and above all sobriety were given important places. In a letter to Suger of St-Denis Bernard wrote 'C'est ainsi qu'un chevalier valeureux, un chef dévoué et fort, lorsqu'il voit les siens lâcher pied, décimés sous les coups de l'ennemi, préfère à la fuite une mort certaine...' (*34*, p.209), which aptly summarises Vivien's position at the start of the battle, just as his assertion that with God's grace his troop of twenty can still defeat the Saracens (ll.572–73) finds an echo in St Bernard's words, quoting Maccabees, 'qu'il Lui est facile de disperser une foule innombrable sous les coups d'une poignée d'hommes' (*34*, p.204).

This spirit of the new knighthood which invests the first part of *ChG*, displacing all previous models of heroism in favour of a code of heroic sacrifice in the name of the Crusade, may also account for the introduction of the refrain referring to 'vespers' and for the contrast originally established between Tedbalt's sacrilegious attitude to the office and Guillaume's and Vivien's piety. Since they were monks, both Templars and Hospitalers were required to attend the offices by their *Rules* (*91*, p.170), and no more succinct way could be found of reminding the audience of the distinction between the new heroism and the old than the hammer blows of a refrain constantly reminding them of the shortcomings of the 'frivolous homicides' represented by Tedbalt and his kind who prove so inapt to perform the work of the *milites Christi*.

G1: War and the Poetics of Suffering

That suffering should be considered an inherent part of the battlefield experience inspiring a sense of horror and loss in the public observing it at second hand is a modern attitude probably inspired by the first photographic reports from the Crimea and the American Civil War. Whatever its origins it was undoubtedly sharpened by the writings of Sassoon, Owen and others during the First World War. Such an attitude is alien to most epic poetry, which tends to share that exultation in warfare exhibited by Bertrand de Born in his poem 'Be'm platz lo gais tems de Pascor' ('I love the merry season of Easter') in which he describes his delight in the sight of a camp, in causing panic among merchants, in the clash of arms and the booty to be won (*30*, pp.224–27).

That is not to say that images of anguish are totally absent from epic poetry. In the *Iliad* Achilles's reaction to the death of Patroclus, and the final scene in which he presents Hector's body to Priam are cases in point. In the Old French epic we have Oliver blinded by blood striking feebly at his companion, and Roland's own sense of compassion for his dying men (*17*, ll.1851–65; 1989–2009) or Bernier's mother and her nuns roasting alive in the burning convent of Origny, and the desperate flight of Ernaut, whose horse floundering in the mud at Origny leaves him an easy victim for Raoul de Cambrai (*32*, ll.1299–1352; 2595ff.). Yet this sense of suffering is not the predominant tone of these poems, and it was not on such grounds that Aristotle equated epic with tragedy. On the contrary, despite what we would consider as the bleakness of much of his material, the poet of the older section of *Raoul* (*32*, ll.1–5374) calls his poem a 'chançon de joie et de baudor' (*32*, l.1), echoing the sentiment and spirit of Bertrand, and showing an

attitude to warfare summarised in the case of *Aliscans* by Nelly
Andrieux-Reix as 'Récit épique de bataille = récit de fête' (*40*,
p.11). The growth in human stature of both Achilles and
Charlemagne as a result of their perception of fatality and suffering
goes hand-in-hand with a loss of mythic stature, and illustrates well
the Aristotelian concept of the tragic affiliations of epic. Yet the
Greek and the Old French poems are not shy to offer a view of war
which exults in deeds of arms and even simplistic triumphalism.

In this respect *G1* stands out as a notable exception to the
general rule. Suffering, as both physical pain and mental anguish, is
shown in this poem to be intrinsic to the battlefield experience. This
comes out most clearly in the account of the death of Vivien, which
contrasts starkly with the deaths of both Roland and Isembart (in
Gormont et Isembart), in which the repentant renegade, like the
untarnished Christian warrior-hero, is granted a peaceful death in
the *locus amoenus* (*66*, pp.183–202) of a shady olive tree,
apparently removed from the scene of strife, although the
fragmentary nature of the poem prevents our being sure that this is
his actual end (*13*, ll.655–61). Not that pain and suffering are totally
absent in any of these cases. Prior to his repentance Isembart rides
alone across the battlefield, and is hacked down by four anonymous
warriors who set on him simultaneously (*13*, ll.613–28); in the
Roland, although the hero seems exempt from wounds other than
the self-inflicted injuries caused by blowing his Olifant, which are
described in horrifying detail, Oliver and Turpin both suffer, and
die from wounds they have received. Yet like the hero himself, they
are permitted a peaceful death, and Turpin, the archbishop, in
particular is represented in death with the decorative repose of an
alabaster statue (*17*, ll.2249–50). Most importantly, the deaths occur
in the absence of the enemy, and the very formal funerary laments
which Roland pronounces over both of them lends them an air of
ritual drama, which will be the hallmark of Roland's own carefully
choreographed death and translation to Heaven.

It is this hieratic aspect that is missing in the case of Vivien's
death in *G1*. The spiritual dimension of his experience is present in
his prayers of repentance, but these also are unlike those of the other

warriors we have considered, who offer formal confessions, quotations from the funeral rite, and ritual commendations of their souls to God or the Virgin. In contrast, Vivien's first prayer is merely a brief reiteration of that most urgent of needs which he had felt the previous evening in Bourges:

> 'Sainte Marie, virgine pucele,
> tramettez mei, dame, Lowis u Willame!'
> (797–98)

His next two prayers, modelled on those of Christ in Gethsemane, stress by their figural connotations the sense of agony and abandonment in the soul of the hero. Furthermore he is the only hero to pray

> 'garisez mei pur ta sainte merci,
> que ne m'ocient cist felon Sarazin!'
> (815–16)

Such despairing, human weakness would be beneath the invulnerable certainties of a Roland, and even the apostate Isembart has moved beyond the pain of the battlefield to be concerned only, and articulately, with the state of his soul (*13*, ll.634–54). Not that Vivien takes no heed for his salvation, but his concerns are presented in immediate physical and psychological terms. The rest of the *laisse* in which he asked to be spared (the equivalent to Christ's asking that the cup pass from Him: Matthew, 27: 39) is concerned with his repentance for this specific weakness:

> 'Respit de mort, sire, ne te dei jo rover,
> car a tei meisme ne la voilsis pardoner.'
> (823–24)

There is, however, no hint here of the ritual *prière du plus grand péril* found in so many *chansons de geste* (*67*); rather we are confronted by Vivien's obsessive sense of his own inadequacy, seen

in his long-drawn comparison between himself and Guillaume
(ll.828–34), and in his recurrent fear that he might be driven to
break his vow and flee from the battle (ll.901–03; 909–12). Indeed
the last words we hear Vivien pronounce in this part of the poem
refer to his 'fear of death' (l.912). Even the sacrilegious and
blaspheming Raoul de Cambrai is spared that, and permitted to
pronounce a brief prayer to the Virgin for his soul's salvation with
his final breath (*32*, l.2952). Moreover, since, at the point at which
his prayers are uttered, Vivien is wandering unhorsed, agonising
with thirst, heat, nausea and fearful wounds (his bowels hanging out
through rips in his belly), and using his sword not as a weapon to
fight the enemy but as a walking-stick, they represent not the
translation of a tactical possibility, but the ultimate anguish of a
mind in torment.

   ChG is unusual, at least in *G1*, in that it concentrates on the
human isolation and suffering of death, while offering no image of
an assured salvation. Vivien's torments, and anguished cry of

>   'Allas, peccable! n'en puis mais...
>   Que me demande ceste gent adverse?'
>   (835–37)

lead not to the transcendent glory of martyrdom, but to the
anonymous and bestial death of a hunted animal (ll.767–68;
860–63). His final resting-place is no *locus amoenus*, merely any
tree by the wayside, where he is dumped so that Christians will not
find him (ll.927–28). The purpose of this is to prevent proper burial
in consecrated ground, the object of Turpin's support for Roland's
desire to recall Charlemagne. This lack of Christian burial would
have had a strong symbolic impact on an early twelfth-century
audience, since, at that time, the ritual of solemn burial within
church (and preferably monastic) precincts was still held to be
necessary to ensure the soul's safe passage to paradise in the
absence of a fully elaborated doctrine of purgatory (*91*, pp.61–63,
116–17). Thus Vivien's death is one of simple blind faith, and not
part of a reciprocal, feudal, contract with the Deity, as is Roland's.

This view holds only for *G1*, and is totally overthrown in *G2*. When Guillaume finally discovers Vivien's body (ll.2011–13), the décor and atmosphere are those of the paradisal 'hero's resting-place'. Instead of a polluted stream filled with human offal and an anonymous tree beside a track, we find a clear spring and the olive tree of traditional idealised epic scenery (*66*, pp.183–202). Although Vivien's body is still covered with wounds, these are now of merely epic severity 'Parmi le cors out quinze plaies tels, / de la menur fust morz uns amirelz' (ll.2014–15), designed to emphasise the super-human qualities of the hero who has borne them. Moreover, Vivien is not yet dead, but dies only after making a formal confession of faith and receiving the sacrament, taking a portion of bread conserved from the Last Supper itself (ll.2027–28). This scene, which is played out at even greater length in *Aliscans*, but where the host has a humbler and more 'realistic' origin on 'l'autel saint Germein' (*7*, l.959), belongs solely to the *G2-Aliscans* tradition, replacing the bleak anguish of the older poem with the conventionally reassuring vision of the warrior's death. Even so, the *G2* poet could not escape the force of tradition, since Guillaume fails to remove Vivien's body from l'Archamp, and at the end of the poem he is totally lost to view, except for the brief allusion in the final scene of the poem, when lands attributed to him are passed to Rainoart. If, as is not impossible, the Girard-Guischard interpolator has replaced the return of Vivien's body to Guibourc with that of her renegade nephew's body, then the effect has been to add irony to the tragedy of the original poem.

It is not only the poet's attitude to the death of the hero, but his presentation of war itself which makes *G1* stand out among *chansons de geste*. While not all Old French epic poets made fighting the prime focus of their interest (it is of comparatively minor importance in such diverse poems as *Girart de Roussillon* — quantitatively —, *Ami et Amile*, *Le Charroi de Nîmes* and *PO* — thematically —, and plays no part at all in *Le Pèlerinage de Charlemagne*), they are generally united when they do describe it, in that pain never gives way to horror. Rather, since battles are generally depicted as a series of single combats between champions, punctuated by a generally evoked mêlée, which provides a backdrop for deeds of heroism, the repetitive stylisation of the fighting generates a rhythmic euphoria which negates any sense of individual suffering, even when Christian heroes are dying. Needless to say, the deaths of pagans, even the most bloody, provoke pure exultation.

Of *G1*'s 1980 lines, 1280 (64.7%) are devoted to scenes which occur on the battlefield of l'Archamp. If we divide the poem into two episodes at the death of Vivien, to reflect the structure disrupted by the Girard-Guischard interpolation, we find that the first part has a proportion of 726 out of 931 lines (78%), a remarkably high proportion, which could be increased again, if we considered the flight of Tedbalt and Esturmi to be part of the battlefield sequence. Yet, despite this massive concentration on events on or near the battlefield, the audience 'sees' very little fighting. At the very beginning Vivien kills a pagan with the lance on which he has just raised his pennon (ll.314–26) and Girard mimics this action (actually killing two pagans) on his return from pursuing and humiliating Tedbalt and Esturmi (ll.436–46). Both these deeds belong to the stylised world of conventional epic warfare, although they lack the formal element of the challenge. However, any expectations they have raised in the audience that what follows will be a traditional epic are frustrated, as no further fighting as such is depicted for nearly four hundred lines. Instead we find scenes which would be worthy of a modern war poet.

The enemy suddenly become an unseen menace, and are all the more threatening because of that. The focus shifts from direct combat to the results of conflict: we see Vivien and Girard wandering through the battlefield, not slaying hosts of Saracens but witnessing the suffering of their own men. Vivien looks across a plain towards the 'fere compaigne / des mielz de France' (ll.474–75) assembled for battle, but sees only 'Mult...de els gisir a tere' (l.476); next thirty horns sound the rally and seven hundred men carrying bloodstained swords form up to withstand a further attack (ll.489–92); going further on he finds three hundred of his fellow countrymen drenched in their own blood with their bowels hanging out (ll.494–99). Then the young companions-in-arms come across a sort of field station, where the less wounded struggle to bring aid to the more seriously maimed and snapped-off lance-shafts are being   strapped to shattered arms to give the wounded some chance of fighting on (ll.517–27). Finally the pair survey the dead:

> Tels set .c. homes trovent de lur terre
> entre lur pez trainant lur bowele;
> parmi lur buches issent fors lur cerveles
> et de lur escuz se covrent sur l'erbe.
> Trubles unt les vis et palles les meisseles,
> turnez les oilz qui lur sistrent as testes.
> Geinent et crient cels qui les almes i perdent.
>
> (529–35)

The impact of this litany of suffering and death, already unique in the Old French epic, and which rises to a surprising, audible crescendo in the noted groans and screams of the dying, is intensified by the shift of viewpoint away from an omniscient narrator to the partial perspective of a character. This technique, used to such acclaimed effect by Stendhal in *La Chartreuse de Parme* and Tolstoy in *War and Peace*, has the effect of removing any objectivising distance from the events and plunging the audience into the chaos of the battlefield. However, whereas the nineteenth-century novelists used non-combatants to register the appalling carnage of Waterloo and Borodino, the *G1* poet has magnified the effect by having the disaster recorded through the eyes of a commander, who is powerless to stop the butchery, and whose increasingly despairing appeals for the presence of Guillaume or Louis are echoed by the poet's interjected apostrophes to the 'dolente presse' (ll.449; 456; 695; 701), the 'doleruse presse' (l.612), the 'dolent champ' (ll.472; 703) which act as a structuring refrain.

Vivien may try to encourage his men by calling on them to avenge their fallen comrades, and not break their word to the dead, but he has to admit to the fallen that 'N'avrez mes mirie pur nul

home de terre' (ll.502; 537). The only hope he can offer them is the
conventional one

> 'car saint Estephne ne les altres martirs
> ne furent mieldres que serrunt tut icil,
> qui en l'Archamp serrunt pur Deu ocis.'
>
> (545–47)

This martyrdom is highly painful though, as the poet points out,
detailing the slaughter of the French in seven brief lines (ll.553–59).
Thus, when Vivien insists that with God's aid they can still win, his
men's reply is first a disbelieving 'A la Deu beneiçun!' (l.565), then
the assertion that God has forgotten them (l.574). But these words
are spoken by men ready to give up the fight, and who only return to
the field because they can find no safe way through the enemy's
lines. It then remains only for the poet to tally baldly the slaughter
of the rump of the troop before embarking on the long description of
Vivien's final agony.

The second sequence in *G1*, the Girard-Guischard interpolation, presents a quite different tone, while still generally eschewing
battle-description. The second battle at l'Archamp is passed over in
cold résumé (ll.1120–28) before the poet concentrates on the deaths
of Girard and Guischard, which, if painful, are presented essentially
to mark the symbolic contrast between the faithful Christian and the
apostate. These deaths are also thematically linked to Vivien's by
the way that each man calls out for wine, or water from the polluted
stream (Girard, l.1159; Guischard, l.1195). This motif also recalls
the scene at the 'field station' where the wounded

> dunc but del vin qu'il ad el champ trové.
> Qui n'out de tel, si but del duit troblé,
> et sains homes en donent as nafrez.
>
> (524–26)

This time there is a lighter tone, defiant in the case of Girard, ironic
in the case of Guischard, since his drink will fortify him for the

journey back to Cordoba, which he regrets ever having left. The final irony is visited on Guillaume, however, since he is forced by his vow to Guibourc to carry the apostate's body back to Barcelona, abandoning the two faithful heroes, Girard and Vivien, on the field.

The third battle is, indeed, unlike either of the previous two, and resembles more closely than they did the conventional battle-description of the *chansons de geste* (*81*). There is an opening address to the troops followed by a firm concentration on the exploits of Guillaume and Gui as they combine to rout the pagans after a hard fight which reaches its climax in the death of Desramé. Yet this narration is not wholly traditional, nor devoid of parodic intent (see below, pp.104–06), as Guillaume hardly cuts a heroic figure, surrounded by pagans and on the point of being killed himself when Gui, fortified by a good drink of wine, comes to his rescue. Vivien's role has been divided between two characters, and tragedy has turned to comedy, as Gui first rescues his uncle, and then in a most unchivalrous way, cuts off the pagan commander's head.

These later episodes merely throw into greater relief the sense of suffering, which is all-pervading in the Vivien episode, and which extends beyond the battle-field proper. Girard's journey to Barcelona (ll.696–744) is marked by many of the same features as Vivien's agony. We have seen that Girard's death is linked to Vivien's by the theme of thirst and the polluted stream, and the same motif appears during the journey to Barcelona. After fighting his way through the ranks of Saracens over a space of five leagues, and then walking fifteen more following the death of his horse, he finds nothing to drink but salt sea-water (ll.705–13). Another motif linking the two warriors is the use of the sword as a walking-stick, with a strong emphasis not only on the scabbard's being filled with gore, but on the fact that the noble point of the sword is pressed to the ground

> Totes ses armes out guerpi li Frans,
> fors sul s'espee, dunt d'acer fu li brant,
> tote vermeille des le helt en avant,

> l'escalberc pleine de foie et de sanc.
> Nue la porte, si s'en vait suz puiant
> et la mure vers terre reposant...
> sa nue espee al destre poig portant,
> devers la mure si s'en vait apoiant.
>   (731–41)

cf.

> En sa main destre porte [Vivien] d'ascer un brant,
> tut fu vermeil des le helz en avant,
> l'escalberc pleine de feie et de sanc:
> devers la mure s'en vait apuiant.
> La sue mort le vait mult destreignant
> et il se sustent contreval de sun brant.
>   (888–93)

Now in *ChG* the arming motif itself consistently includes the unfamiliar feature that the sword when strapped on has its point to the ground (factually true, but usually ignored by poets, cf. ll.135, 224, 1112, 1500). The traditional symbolism of the sword includes notions of brightness, glory and heroic virtue, which are supported by the sword, like the lance with its attendant banner, being depicted pointing to the sky. Here we have quite the opposite. Not that the characters are being belittled, indeed the inverted sword stained with blood bears even more resemblance to the Cross than normal, so that the status of the two young warriors as martyrs is being underlined.

The use of the motif in Girard's case is all the more significant in that he is not about to die, so that his 'martyrdom' is purely symbolic and is read in the light of the sympathetic equivalence established between himself and Vivien. The point in the narration in which the motif is introduced in each case is also important. In Vivien's case it occurs after his horse has been killed and when he is reduced *de facto* from the status of knight to that of foot soldier. Similarly Girard is portrayed in this way after he has shed his armour piece by piece, jettisoning what cannot be of help to Vivien at l'Archamp. In doing this Girard is abandoning the role of knight adopted for the nonce, when he purloined the arms of the disgraced Tedbalt (ll.384–85). His actual status is that of squire, and Vivien asked him on his return to the battlefield how long he had been a knight, revealing some surprise at his transformation. His reversion to the role of unarmed squire, after his brief, and brave, but futile service as a knight, completes the curve established in his self-arming. In removing the armour Girard adopts an order which may appear realistic (spear, shield, helmet, mail shirt) but which is really just the converse of the traditional description of the arming of a knight (mail shirt, helmet [sword], shield, [spear], ll.1075–78; 1498–1502), and which will be followed when Girard is finally armed officially by Guillaume and Guibourc in Barcelona.

The oppression which weighs on the young man during his journey is felt through the litany of laments he utters as he jettisons each piece of equipment, repeating the words 'peises' (ll.716; 720), 'vas apesant' (l.727), 'estunes' (l.723) in a formulaic incantation. The atmosphere is further darkened as the scene invites comparison with Girard's self-arming, at which point the poet treated the audience to a conventional epic history for the arms, paying particular attention to the shield decorated with Arabian gold, captured from a Hungarian in a battle at Gerona (or Saragossa: cf. below, pp.117–18), when Vivien killed Alderufe and the twelve sons of Borel, and passed via Guillaume to Tedbalt. When Girard dons it the poet remarks 'uncore hui l'averad mult prozdome a la gule' (l.381). Thus, when Girard throws this shield away as so much encumbering scrap metal, we see that Tedbalt and Esturmi's boastful cowardice has brought to nothing a whole history of Christian Frankish heroism.

The immediate cause of Girard's stripping himself of the signs of his knighthood is the great heat. The poet has been at pains to point out that the month is May, and the heat therefore intense (l.709). In fact in the near contemporary lyric, both Occitan courtly love songs, and northern spring songs, May is considered a warm, rather than hot month, conducive to all manifestations of renewal

(*69*, pp.163–93), so that the two parts of the motif do not seem to fit together here. The month may have been chosen to provide a reference to the Feast of St William of Gellone (28th May), who is normally considered to be the prototype of Guillaume in the poem. The great heat provides an independent network of symbols, whose significance becomes apparent only as the song unfolds. At the beginning Tedbalt and his army move and fight by day. Only later do we learn that the heat is so intense that Guillaume and his army move by night when it is cool (l.1087), a rationalising explanation of the Girard-Guischard interpolator. This same heat, which has burned the surrounding country into an arid waste and dried up the refreshing streams, so that Vivien has to drink polluted salt water, and Girard can find nothing to drink, has left a mud hole into which Tedbalt and Esturmi can trample their pennons (ll.269; 274) and seems to smile on the pagans, who repeatedly picnic and stroll by the shore while waiting for a favourable wind for setting sail (ll.1095–97; 1685–90). Indeed the symbolism of light and dark seems to be inverted in this poem. All Christian activity — Tedbalt's disastrous, drunken boasting, Girard's delivery of his message, Guillaume's two failed attempts to avenge Vivien — begins or climaxes at or after vespers, the last main office of the day, before night falls. Although most fighting seems to happen in daylight, the three-day battle of the Girard-Guischard section signals continuous slaughter until just before prime (the dawn office — l.1123) emphasising the rule of darkness in this episode. Only Rainoart in *G2* will rouse the troops in time to have them on the battlefield for prime. By contrast the arrival of the pagan hordes is suffused in a threatening brightness (ll.232–33) which negates the optimistic symbolism of the *Roland* (*48*).

Darkness is the very element in which the heroes must move in *ChG*, and the light of heavenly day has been transformed into the heat of Hell. The vast size and ill-defined boundaries of the battlefield, stretching seemingly from the gates of Bourges through the mouth of the Gironde to Barcelona (and, in *G2*, east to Orange and back up to Tours), together with the heat and aridity, present us with a truly apocalyptic image of war, inherited partly from ancestral Indo-European epic models (*71*, pp.246–65), and partly from the Bible. The battlefield itself has become a protagonist, and the world a battlefield on which the *miles Christi*, represented by the monk-like and ascetic Vivien, must sacrifice himself for a good he cannot see amidst all the physical tortures of bodily pain and the mental anguish of doubt and fear. This image is rewritten in a more conventional form in the Girard-Guischard interpolation, and with a more sophisticated wit in the Gui episode. The whole edifice will be swept away in *G2* with the arrival on the scene of Rainoart, and the more comfortable view, for western chivalry, of the hero as *Matamoros* ('Moor Slayer').

G2 or La Chanson de Rainoart

With the unexpected, and unannounced, arrival of Rainoart into the poem (l.2648) the entire text receives a new orientation. Although much of what passes in this episode has been considered essentially comic, with that comedy revolving around the personality and exploits of the new hero (*102*, pp.42–43, 57–61, 99), we are, perhaps, more properly dealing with an ebullient euphoria. The whole episode, from Vivien's idealised death in a heavily emphasised state of grace to the final victory of the Christians and the formal incorporation of Rainoart into the Christian feudal community as Vivien's 'heir', can be read as the element which defines the whole of *ChG* as a comedy, in the technical sense that its narrative line describes a rising parabola from the disasters announced in Bourges to the securing of peace and the destruction of the invaders: from a state of distress to a state of beatitude (for a discussion of comedy as humour in *G1* and *G2*, as well as in *PO*, see below, pp.100ff.). Symbolically it could be read either as the regeneration of feudal society (*39*; *64*) or as a model of spiritual salvation, from the 'fall' of Tedbalt and Esturmi, through the sacrifice of Vivien, to the extension of the Kingdom of God, represented by the token of Rainoart's baptism. The problem that subsists with each of these readings is that Guillaume, the hero of the song according to ll.4–11, is evinced from the central role we should expect him to play.

That role is taken on in *G2* by the character regularly referred to by critics as 'le géant Rainouart' (*7*, p.366). However there is no clear indication in *G2* that the young Saracen is of anything other than 'normal' heroic stature. Jeanne Wathelet-Willem refers to the character in *G2* as 'un jeune homme particulièrement costaud' (*130*, p.289), and Gustav Adolf Beckmann distinguishes the explicit gigantism of Rainoart in *Aliscans* from the implications of gigantism to be read into *G2* (*46*, p.56). There are in fact only two allusions to his size in the poem. The first occurs on his entrance, when he is portrayed as having big feet (l.2650); the second comes when Rainoart is explaining to Bertrand that he cannot control the *tinel* when making a normal, descending, stroke (ll.3102–07). His explanation includes the line 'Grosse est la brace qui me tient al costé' (l.3104), which is not easy to interpret in context, but which may be taken as meaning that he cannot control his weapon despite the size of his arms. It is in fact only in *Aliscans* that he is described as being abnormally large when he first comes on the scene in person:

> Grant ot le cors et regart de sengler,
> En tote France n'ot si grant bacheler,
> Ne si fort home por un grant fés lever...
> Si grant fés porte, sanz mençonge conter,
> Une charrete avroit mout a porter.
>
> (*7*, 3528–33)

This impression is reinforced in *Aliscans* by the justification which Louis gives for not having his scullion baptised: 'Por sa grandor nel poi onques amer' (*7*, l.3579), which here must be taken as a reference to physical size, since in this account the young man has refused to reveal his parentage. In *G2* this explanation is given by Rainoart himself at the end of the poem, where he declares unequivocally that it is on account of his noble birth, and particularly because he is afraid of his father, that Louis has

Rainoart condemned to a life in the kitchen (ll.3537–44). A third possible allusion (that the tub used as a font to baptise him was big enough for four peasants to bathe in, ll.3491–92) seems quite out of keeping in its elementary humour with what has gone before, and might be imputable to a later scribe. It is notable that gigantism is totally absent from the equivalent scene in *Aliscans*, although Rainoart stands head and shoulders above the warriors around him (7, l.7892).

There are, of course, a number of features in the presentation of Rainoart that would lead later writers to assume gigantism in him from the beginning. These are mainly concerned with the size of his 'club', to use that general term for the moment to designate his preferred weapon. When Rainoart forgets his *tinel* on starting out for Orange (ll.2723–24), Guillaume offers to have him another one cut from a forest tree 'a ta mesure, et long et quarré' (l.2739). The apparent identification of the size and girth of Rainoart with that of his weapon is an illusion, which also afflicts Guillaume. The first half of the line, meaning 'big enough for you', is not genuinely reversible, and Rainoart is quick to point out that it is not the size of the weapon but its intrinsic nature which is important:

> 'Suz ciel n'ad bois u il fust recovré.
> Ben a set anz que jo oi le tinel
> en la quisine de Loun la cité;
> unc nel vi freindre ne desercler.'
> (2741–44)

Rainoart like his 'stick', as other characters repeatedly call it in denigration, remains unbroken in body or spirit by the seven years which both have served together in Louis's kitchen. The use of the 'mystical' number seven indicates, as it does in much twelfth-century literature where it is effectively reduced to a cliché to alert the public to the imminent recounting of important developments, that the period of apprenticeship or trial is over and the essence of the hero is about to be made manifest.

The inability of the Flemish knight sent by Guillaume to retrieve it is also symptomatic of the essential identity of the hero and his weapon. Granted that the knight is sent alone to fetch it, while the scullions who make off with it in earlier and later episodes are of indeterminate number, so that combined physical force may be in question, but Rainoart's reaction on being cursed by the Fleming who could not move it is instructive:

> Dist Reneward: 'Mé i covient aler.
> Ja ne vendrat pur nul home qui seit nez
> se les meins braz ne l'unt aportez.'
>
>   (2761–63)

According to this statement it is not a question of strength but of election: the *tinel* will come of its own volition for the right man. This is a common motif in world folk and hero tales, its best-known manifestation in European literature being Arthur's sword, Excalibur, which only the king can draw from the stone; it also figures in the Chinese Bhuddist allegory, *Monkey*, where the hero's brass-banded iron staff, originally a pillar of the world, can be taken and used only by the elect hero, Monkey, himself.

But what is the nature of this weapon? It is commonly referred to as a 'club' or 'massue' by critics, who have seen Rainoart as a variant on Hercules (*108*), and this is the interpretation given to the word by most editors and translators when it appears in *Roland*, where Baligant's spear-shaft is described 'grosse cume uns fust de tinel' (*17*, l.3153). However, the gloss is inadequate in this context, where 'fust' is a worked shaft fitted to the lance-head, while a club, as represented regularly in the iconography of Hercules or in the Bayeux Tapestry, is formed from a single piece of wood and of an irregular shape that makes it unsuited to stand as an image of a lance-shaft. This weapon has recently been reinterpreted in the light of a common meaning of *tinel* as 'little tub' to make of it a barrel, and of Rainoart himself a god of plenty (*125*). Now, while this interpretation clearly cannot be right because of the way in which Rainoart is described as carrying and using it, the association with

barrels or buckets is correct. Jeanne Wathelet-Willem was the first
to gloss Rainoart's instrument as 'porte-seaux' (*129*), and it may be
because the scullion's tool was consecrated as a weapon by Rainoart
that, in *PO*, two Saracens appear at a convenient moment carrying
wine in containers suspended from a *tinel*, which Guillaume
appropriates as a weapon (*PO*, *AB* ll.1631–39). Now it is only in
Aliscans that this identification is made explicit by Louis describing
Rainoart at work: '.IIII. mui d'eve li ai veü porter / a un tinel...' (*7*,
ll.3583–84); in *G2* its nature is left vague, except that it is clearly
manufactured, since it is bound up with iron bands to stop the wood
splitting (l.2744). The process of manufacture (shaping and smooth-
ing with an adze, hardening in fire, having the bands fitted by a
smith, waxing) is spelled out in *Aliscans*, where Rainoart makes a
new *tinel*, specifically for use in the coming battle (*7*, ll.3749–63).
The double link with an item of manufacture and domesticity may
explain why he refuses a 'raw' club cut from a tree, while at the end
of *ChG*, when he supplies himself with a new weapon, it is likewise
an item originally fashioned for another, peaceful, purpose: the
ridge-pole of a peasant's hut (ll.3410–14).

Nor did the intrinsic link of the *tinel* with fire escape the poet
of the *PO*. The occasion referred to above, when Guillaume purloins
a *tinel* to transform himself into a *post facto* prefiguration of
Rainoart, is the second such passage in the poem. On the first
occasion he looks around for a weapon and sees a *tinel* 'Qui por feu
fere i estoit aporté' (*AB* l.828). This would make of the *tinel* a mere
log, which is a viable meaning for the Old French word, yet one
which is appropriated for the production of fire: the controlled heat
of civilisation. Guillaume immediately transforms this into an
instrument of destruction, though in the service of 'civilisation' as
viewed by the epic poet. Equally, the use of fire in the manufacture
of the *tinel* in *Aliscans*, where the wood is hardened with fire before
a smith forges and fits the bands, makes manifest the reciprocity of
the relationship between the fire and the tool-weapon. It also
reminds us that the symbolism of fire is highly ambiguous, as
Gaston Bachelard pointed out (*42*, p.19): 'Parmi tous les phéno-
mènes, il est vraiment le seul qui puisse recevoir aussi nettement les

deux valorisations contraires: le bien et le mal. Il brille au Paradis. Il brûle à l'Enfer. Il est douceur et torture. Il est cuisine et apocalypse.'

Nor is it a matter of choice. Both poles are permanently present in the symbolism, as Labbé indicated by attributing to Rainoart the magical capacity to extract martial fury from the culinary (*89*, pp.216–17). This same intrinsic link is seen in the character of Rainoart himself. Scorched by the fire, he is never harmed or diminished by it: it merely releases his fury (ll.2867–70); conversely his first victim in the fight for liberation, the head cook who tries to prevent his leaving, is consumed by his own fire when Rainoart hurls him into it with the force of a blow from his *tinel* (ll.2684–88). That this is a truly epic feat, comparable to the defenestration of Aymon le Vieil in *Le Charroi de Nîmes* (*20*, ll.678–752), is shown by the *gab* which Rainoart pronounces over his fallen foe, ordering him sarcastically to rise and telling him that, like the hobgoblin, he will now be held responsible for all that is lost in the house (ll.2689–91).

It is therefore a mistake to exaggerate the grotesque or 'carnavalesque' aspects of Rainoart (*99*) and to equate him with the 'low' functions of 'third function' heroes (*71*, pp.29–74, esp. 53–58, 71–72). When he turns a spit with his sword strapped on (ll.2854–55), this is less to evoke laughter at incongruity, although that may be a subsidiary effect, than to dramatise the dual nature of the hero. Similarly, when he follows Guillaume and Guibourc into the great hall at Orange with his *tinel* across his shoulders, he is the image of the perfect fool (*57*, pp.54–55), so that, while the uninitiated consider him a dolt and fear he will kill them, Guillaume's simple description of him as 'uns joefnes hom que Deus m'ad amené' (l.2818) stresses both his inherent purity and the sacred nature of his mission. Like Gui he emerges from the fire to save Christendom; like Havelok the Dane, he is inseparable from the holy fire of his nobility which burns within him, waiting only the moment to manifest itself. Like Havelok he is a mixture of Fair Unknown and Repressed or Unpromising Hero; less an example of the World Upside-Down, than of Nature triumphing over a Nurture imposed by the treacherous and pusillanimous (*49*, pp.86–88).

 This is not to say that Rainoart, even in *G2*, does not possess comic traits, but his exploits have an underlying seriousness of purpose and symbolism which transmutes potentially destructive comedy into celebratory euphoria. His first true exploit is the release of Bertrand and the other prisoners from the Saracen ships (ll.3023 ff.), which belongs only to the *G2-Aliscans* tradition. Its significance is underlined by the series of evocations in which Guillaume either laments their captivity or bases a request for military aid on it (ll.2254–58; 2346–55; 2466–67; 2484–86; 2519–21). In this part of the poem the fate of the prisoners is placed on a par with the death of Vivien; indeed, if we compare the ten lines (2346–55) devoted to describing Bertrand's fate with the single line (2342) allotted to Vivien, we might well conclude that it is more important. This importance arises from the established theme of the release of prisoners (by Guillaume in *Le Couronnement de Louis* or Lancelot in Chrétien's *Le Chevalier de la Charrete*) which regularly carries overtones of salvation and the Harrowing of Hell. Although that part of the motif is underplayed here, the prefatory killing of Ailred, guardian and owner of the ship (ll.3016–22), the reference to the tortures inflicted by Malagant (l.3140) and the return to the hill on which Guillaume is positioned in what amounts to a triumphal procession, with Rainoart clearing a path four carts wide for the Christians to ride along (ll.3128–32), provides a schematic framework of allusions to the Christological legend supported by the ascensional movement from the depths of the prison, across fresh grass to the heights where Guillaume is found.

 The narrative world of *G2* remains sufficiently topsy-turvy, however, for this to mark not the culmination but the start of Rainoart's heroic activity. His killing of Gloriant de Palerne is greeted by Guillaume with the recognition that he is worthy to be a knight, and the promise of lands and a noble wife. There follows a series of three duels in which Rainoart has to rescue the Narbonnais from destruction by Tabur de Canaloine (a veritable image of Hell's

Mouth who seeks to swallow up the Christians), the Amirail de Balan (armed with a flail, whose agricultural associations make him an exact, but diabolic, equivalent of Rainoart, since his arrival is referred to as Doomsday) and Aildré (Rainoart's uncle). It is as a result of killing his uncle that Rainoart breaks his *tinel* and 'accidentally' finds the sword with which he effectively wins the battle at the same moment as his essence as a knight is revealed. This accidental finding of the sword, which he has been carrying ever since Guibourc strapped it on in Orange, is comparable to Perceval's divination of his name (*28*, ll.3359–61). Unlike Perceval, however, whose discovery of his essence comes at the depths of his misfortunes and marks the start of his rehabilitation, Rainoart, despite some insults to come, is transformed in a moment of triumph. His being forgotten at the victory feast is a mere *peripeteia* deferring the final celebration of the unity and extension of the Christian community. This may be inspired by the traditional motif of the vengeance exacted by a supernatural being — fairy, magician or giant — for being forgotten at a celebration he or she has helped to bring about, and who can only be placated by a suitable offer of food (cf. *120*, 3, p.71 [F361.1 – 361.2.1]; 5, p.133 [N812.0.1]).

This steady rise of Rainoart to his apotheosis inevitably has as a counterweight the decline of other heroes, older in the epic tradition, like Bertrand, Gui and Guillaume. Guillaume's nephews, his effective right-hand men in so many poems, and, in the case of Gui, the ultimate victor of l'Archamp in the revised version of *G1*, are totally eclipsed in *G2*. Indeed the whole Narbonnais clan, whose solidarity normally guarantees their triumph, have to be rescued by Rainoart, who becomes the sole focus of heroic activity, and effectively of salvation (*77*, pp.34–40; *64*). The establishment of the new hierarchy is exemplified in the episode in which Guielin is rescued from certain death at the hands of Tabur de Canaloine by Guillaume, who in turn has to be rescued by Rainoart (ll.3170–201). Guillaume himself proves to be a worse overlord even than Louis. Not only does he fail to avenge Vivien, but he is incapable of ensuring victory and the safety of his men on the field. Finally he fails to reward the architect of the Christian victory until forced to it by threats of retaliation. Even then it is Guibourc who, in a unique presentation of a sister-brother bond (*87*, pp.111–13), effects the final reconciliation and elevation of Rainoart, as the pair encapsulate the complete renewal of Christendom symbolised by the redeemed Narbonnais, with Guillaume relegated to the role of Guibourc's husband and Rainoart's brother-in-law.

This redemption involves the reintegration into the poem of several characters 'lost' to the action at various stages of *G1* and at the beginning of *G2* (see above, pp.20–21). This effect is also seen in the multiple 'restarts' imposed by the succession of revisers of *G1*. Throughout the song events reduplicate themselves. Guillaume attempts to remove Vivien from the field, having previously carried home Guischard, at which time Guibourc assumes that it is Vivien's body that has been recovered. In fact (in the surviving text) he is not found until we are into *G2*, when he is promptly 'lost' again, so that the end of *G2* effectively mimics the end of *G1* in respect of the fate of the poem's first hero. The hinge of the extant song is marked by Guillaume's double duel with Desramé and Alderufe, and each return to Barcelona/Orange involves a testing of the hero's personality, as each return to l'Archamp finds the pagans indulging in the same picnic and 'tourism' while they await a favourable wind. The assumed clumsiness and incompetence of these revisers, and particularly of the one responsible for sewing *G1* to *G2* (*72*, 1, pp.146–48), might lead one to suppose that these effects were the result of pure accident. The sheer number of such reduplications and restarts, however, invites the conclusion that at some stage accident has been incorporated into art, and that a key redactor (possibly the one who produced the extant version) transferred the principle of epic composition from the microcosm of the *laisse* to the macrocosm of the episode. As a sequence of *laisses similaires* imposes an atmosphere of lyric contemplation on the forward march of narrative, so the exploitation of *épisodes similaires* focuses attention on the impasse of traditional heroism, and even, in *G2*, of the sacrificial heroism of the military orders in the 'new Europe' of the late twelfth century. This impasse is broken by the exploitation at the level of the poem of another jongleur's technique, that of *reprise bifurquée* (when two *laisses* have similar beginnings but different endings; cf. *115*, pp.80–82). Using what I would term *épisodes bifurqués*, the poet has Rainoart destroy the boats (ll.3006–13, 3338–39) from which he had previously released the prisoners while, on that occasion, leaving intact the vessels in which the pagans had repeatedly failed to make good their escape (ll.3026–79). This allows a satisfactory closure for the poem as a whole. In this way a mode of composition which may have begun as a happy accident is systematised to highlight the timeless and transcendental nature of the Christian victory.

It is, of course, inherent in this text that the apparent message of the poem is subverted by its own content. The hero is, after all, unbaptised and has never entered a church. He is a highly dangerous being in the age of 'heresies' that marked the intellectual ferment of the twelfth century, and, if his final integration into conventional Christian and aristocratic society seems to mark a triumph for that society and a promise of new energy in the period following the *débâcle* of the Second Crusade, it is achieved at the expense of every ideal that the traditional society of feudal solidarity and warrior heroism had stood for.

2. La Prise d'Orange

The Epic Component

Whatever views may have been expressed in modern times about the hybrid nature of the poem (*76*; *90*, pp.131–76), in the manuscripts *PO* is presented as a *chanson de geste*, firmly incorporated into the fabric of the Guillaume Cycle (*65*; *72*, 2, pp.255–58), and as such will have raised expectations in the audience which can only have been met, or challenged, by the exploitation of narrative and poetic features associated with the epic. The formal features of poetic composition will be dealt with in the next chapter; the present one will be concerned with narrative motifs.

The audience's expectations as to what they are about to hear are established in two *laisses* constituting a prologue in both redactions *AB* and *C*, which clearly link the poem to the rest of the cycle, by referring to key moments of Guillaume's career, but presented in a rather enigmatic fashion. While this prologue links *PO* structurally to the rest of the cycle by the nature of its contents, it is distinct from that which opens *Le Couronnement de Louis* (which offers only a general statement about Guillaume's sufferings at the hands of the pagans) or that to *Le Charroi de Nîmes* (which highlights the capture of Nîmes and Orange and the battle with Corsolt). The items singled out on this occasion are his depositing his arms on the altar at Brioude (cf. *Le Moniage Guillaume, 21, Première Rédaction*, ll.71–111), and the capture of Nîmes. However, the first allusion is prefaced by an obscure reference to 'Icil…qui en vont a Saint Gile' (*AB*, l.7), who will see the weapons at Brioude. The latter sanctuary, associated with the saint who 'recorded' the events at Roncevaux and played a signal part in the legend of Charlemagne (*14*, ll.2309–3358; *37*, 1, pp.233–35), also figures in the legend of Guillaume, who captured it from rebels in *Le Couronnement de Louis* (*24, AB* ll.2009–16) and following a pilgrimage there had the vision which determined his capture of Nîmes (*20*, ll.543–79). Unlike the other prologues, then, this one works by indirect allusion, calling on the audience's knowledge of the material to make implicit links with the epic biography of Guillaume.

The poet uses the rest of his epic motifs and themes in much the same way. Although some, like the heroes under siege in a tower from Saracens, with or without the added motif of the 'enamoured princess' (*126; 52*), occur in a broad range of poems, others gain their full impact only by the intertextual references they establish within the cycle of Garin de Monglane or beyond. This is most obvious with the capture of the town itself, which, for a twelfth-century audience, may well have been received in a context presupposing knowledge of up to three earlier versions.

One way in which the extant poem links back into these earlier versions is in the presence of Bertrand among the younger generation present at the battle 'desuz Orenge' (*ChG*, ll.667–76), as detailed by Vivien in *G1*. Guïelin, of course, has no place in Vivien's memories of this battle, since he is the perpetual child of the cycle and is being used contemporaneously in that role in *ChG*, where he is called variously 'Gui', 'Guiot' and 'Guiotun', and possibly 'Guielin' (see above, pp.20–21), the name 'Guïelin' also being used for Guillaume's youngest nephew in *Aliscans*. Indeed, the popularity of this young character is such that poets could not resist re-using him, attributing different fathers to him and playing on the numerous diminutive suffixes that could be appended to the basic name, to the great confusion of most modern scholars who, having received a 'positivist' education, insist on treating the various 'Gui' who turn up regularly in the 'Guillaume' epics as 'separate characters' (*131*, 1, pp.534–36, 538–40; *86*, pp.108–09, 'Narbonnais Genealogy'). It is far from clear, however, that a medieval audience would react in the same way: they could not, for one thing, cross-check fine textual details as we are able to do. It is more likely that, as with the conventionally named character-types of Classical drama, they would have recognised the function and accepted the broad identity of the role and person. It is in that spirit that I see the roles of 'Gui' echoing intertextually between *ChG* and *PO*.

We may nevertheless query whether or not his intervention in the extant *PO* is not an invention of the author of that version, since his presence on the spying expedition has something factitious about it. Guillaume's first intention is to take only Gillebert, recently escaped from imprisonment in Orange and a fluent Arabic speaker, as his companion. However, as soon as Guïelin sees the pair 'blacked up' he gets carried away by the excitement of the project:

> Dist Guïelin: «Par le cors saint Richier,
> A grant merveille estes andui changié;
> Or poëz bien tot le monde cerchier,
> Ne seroiz ja par nul home entercié.
> Mes, par l'apostre qu'en a Rome requiert,
> Ge ne leroie, por les membres tranchier,
> N'aille avec vos, si verrai comment iert.»
>
> (*AB* 382-88)

This decision, which is not challenged by Guillaume, clearly distances Guïelin from the primary purpose of the expedition. He will be there merely to act as assessor of the 'performance' of his elders. In this way his role as acerbic commentator on his uncle's amorous weakness is established from the beginning, although *C* adds a line (*5*, l.354) making him a full participant as a spy, while *D* gives Guillaume an extra line (*5*, l.218) thanking the young man for volunteering which recalls the particular dependence of the older man on the younger in *G1*. His other, more heroic role in the capture of the town becomes apparent only after his arming by Orable (redactions *C* and *D*) or by a mysterious 'dame seconde' (*AB* l.961) and, indeed, after the first imprisonment of the Franks. At that point (*AB* ll.1354–56, 1373), soliciting help in their escape which Orable is already bent on giving, he pledges himself to be Orable's knight, in a way which is clearly not intended by the poet to challenge his uncle's position as lover and future husband of the princess, but which reaffirms the particular relationship of Gui to Guibourc in *G1*.

Bertrand's role, on the other hand, is very much that ascribed to him as a companion in Vivien's reminiscences in *G1*, since he it is who finally kills Arragon, the Saracen commander, and effectively wins the town for his uncle (*AB* ll.1839–44). A final link to the cycle as a whole comes when Guillaume and his companions are besieged in Glorïete, and Arragon makes them the standard military offer of the period of being able to leave under safe conduct, provided they surrender the tower and do not force the pagans to take it by storm. Guillaume's reply evokes a background known from many songs in the cycle (*90*, p.141), in which members of the Narbonnais clan march to the rescue of relatives besieged or otherwise in danger. We see the motif in action very clearly in *G2*, where Guillaume's relatives make good the gap left in the system of feudal interdependence by the emperor's weakness. That Louis is associated with Bernard de Bruban, Garin d'Anseüne and Bueves de Commarchis in this passage (*AB* ll.1090–96) serves as an inter-textual 'flag' providing a shorthand by which the episode can be fitted into a known narrative pattern. We should not fall into the 'realist' trap to which Lachet succumbs when he writes 'Même s'il nomme le roi à plusieurs reprises, à aucun moment il n'envisage sérieusement de solliciter son aide' (*90*, p.147). Nor in a tale of this sort should we consider Guillaume to be undermining clan solidarity by putting his nephews 'at risk' (*90*, p.143), since *PO* belongs to that branch of adventure literature in which the hero and his immediate companions are known to survive unscathed in order to assert the rightness of the audience-community's cause. If ultimately only Bertrand comes to the relief of his uncle in this poem, that is not necessarily to undermine the motif as established in other parts of the cycle, since large sections of the audience would be able to anticipate the reassertion of clan solidarity in *G2* (ll.2538–74), where a number of Guillaume's brothers as well as Aimeri, his father, pledge troops to save Orange, or in *Aliscans* (*7*, ll.2986–3514) in which Aimeri and Hernaut but above all

Hermenjart (Guillaume's mother) and her grand-daughter Aaliz join forces to oblige Louis to send troops.

That such help should be sought, and a messenger dispatched to fetch it, is also a commonplace of the epic. The poem most closely related to the extant *PO* in which it is exploited is *Fierabras* (where Richard de Normandie rides to fetch Charlemagne to the aid of Gui de Bourgogne, Roland and the other peers trapped in Aigremore, *52*, pp.7–9). On this occasion, Gillebert leaves on foot to carry the message, in an improbable sequence, the implications of which within the comic structures of the poem will be discussed below (pp.110–11). What is notable, however, is that whereas much is usually made of the difficulties faced by the messenger in evading the enemy's clutches (as in *G1*, where Girart fights through several leagues on his way to Barcelona, or in the passage of *Fierabras* referred to above) here Gillebert faces no obstacles. It seems as if the poet is simply alluding to known motifs to anchor his tale within a tradition, without bothering to elaborate the details that a full-blown work would require.

We get much the same impression with regard to fighting, at least in the *AB* redaction. The final capture of Orange is recounted in just one *laisse* (60 in *AB*) and barely one hundred lines including the passage through the tunnel to enter Glorïete and the reunion of Bertrand and Guillaume. Although the fighting takes place in the streets of a town, the poet depicts a properly epic cavalry battle, involving tens of thousands of men, which quickly passes to its climax in a duel between Bertrand and Arragon. While this battle between surrogates may be seen as part of the 'démythification' of the hero perceived by Lachet in *PO* (*90*, pp.169–75), it is more likely to form part of the process of civilising the ancient myth of the conquest of Sovereignty (*52*, pp.5–6), and Bertrand's epic sword blow (*AB* ll.1842–44) is presented with a sobriety that defies appeals to parody. What we clearly have in this sequence, as in much else of the poem in the *AB* redaction, is an exercise in *abbreviatio*, about which the poet is quite explicit: 'Que vos iroie le plet plus aloignant?' (*AB* l.1846). This rhetorical procedure of abridgement is handled by allusions, forcing the public to fill in the necessary details. So we have the bulk of the enemy despatched in seventeen lines (*AB* ll.1812–28) before the final duel, which leads to the *abbreviatio* formula, itself a prelude to a couplet 'Mal soit de cel qui en soit eschapant / Desus la terre en cort le ru del sanc' (*AB* ll.1847–48) summarising the battle and evoking, by its use of the definite article to determine 'the river of blood', a tradition stretching (in 'French' epic) from the eleventh-century 'Hague Fragment' (where blood flows in torrents around the besieged Saracen town) to *Raoul de Cambrai* where blood as much as rain turns the battlefield of Origny into quagmire (*32*, ll.2595–96). In both *G1*, in which Gui wades knee-deep in blood (ll.1886–87), and *G2*, where the slaughter is such that the river of blood is deep enough to drive a watermill (ll.2993–94), the motif is already exaggerated to the point of being grotesque.

The *C(E)* redaction takes a much more conventional line. In this version the final capture of the town is spread over 280 lines (*C* ll.1974–2254) with a double series of combats in the town and within the citadel, which we must interpret as being Glorïete. Among the features not found in *AB* are the double duel of Arragon with Bertrand (which remains inconclusive as Arragon is rescued by his men: *C* ll.2013–67) and Guillaume (who finally despatches the pagan commander, making the victory indisputably his own: *C* ll.2237–43). Although the presentation of Guillaume's fight with Arragon is much briefer than that of his nephew with the Saracen king, it does mark a specific climax, particularly when coupled with the victory insult pronounced by Guillaume (*C* ll.2244–47*a*), who asserts the vengeance he has taken for the fallen, including Gillebert, who simply disappears from *AB* once he has shown Bertrand the way into the town. *D*'s rather garbled version (which tries to be more logical in having Bertrand introduced directly into Glorïete and then having the gates opened to admit the bulk of the army on a signal sounded on a horn) does nevertheless support *C* in having Arragon flee never to be seen again once the fighting starts (*D* ll.1538–42). This allows us to suggest that the longer version found in *C* was probably the version in the archetype of the cyclic poem, which *AB*, as we have just seen, has abbreviated, giving transparent rhetorical indicators of the procedure used. The allusive brevity of *AB* may well have had a comic effect on hearers (although that is far from certain), and if it did it would have had the force of a sophisticated wit. The poet is implicitly inviting his audience to agree that there is no need to recount the capture of the town and the decisive duel in detail, since the technique for doing so is a matter of cliché, which the audience can supply for itself.

Arragon's abortive intervention, leading to his death at the hands of Bertrand, likewise offers a brief allusion encapsulating a whole epic tradition. After leaping on his war-horse to confront the invaders he 'Prist un escu qu'il tolli a un Franc' (*AB* l.1832). In this line we are quite unable to tell whether he took it from round the neck of a recently fallen enemy, or from one killed long ago. Whichever it may be, the line evokes a whole history of trophies taken from a fallen enemy, including, in the Guillaume Cycle, the shield that passed from a pagan via Vivien and Guillaume to Tedbalt de Burges and ultimately to Girart (*ChG*, ll.370–81). In a strange way Arragon is given an added epic grandeur here, since unlike in his earlier appearances in the poem he is neither a caricatural monster with talons for hands (*AB* ll.229–33) nor an irascibly misogynistic step-son pouring scorn on his elderly father for marrying a young woman and voicing conventional opinions about his step-mother's supposedly loose morals (*AB* ll.619–29). His rehabilitation as a worthy epic opponent reflects positively on the warrior who vanquishes him, and counteracts his apparent lack of heroic qualities, as presented in the scenes in Nîmes, where he pronounces a totally misplaced lament over the imagined death of Guillaume, and before the walls of Orange, when he despairs of breaking through them, which immediately precede this victory.

This same technique is used to describe the arms given to Guillaume, Guïelin and Gillebert by Orable and her lady-in-waiting (*AB* ll.941–95). The only background supplied for the arms given to Guillaume is that they previously belonged to Tiebaut; handing them over thus stands as a metonymy for his replacement in all his functions by the Frankish hero. The ritual aspect of this arming and

its symbolic import is emphasised by *D*, in which Orable admin-
isters the *colée* to Guillaume with the words

> «Chevaliers soies, Guillelmes au cor neis,
> Sor Sarrazins hardis et redoutés!»
>   (808–09)

as if he were a new knight to whom she is giving a name and a
mission. Guillaume's reply

> «Vostres suis ge volanters et de gré:
> Or me ravés de novel adoubé.»
>   (811–12)

shows his acceptance of his 'new birth' and entry upon the
significant phase of his life. This highly charged 'knighting' thus
acts as a substitute for the actual fight between Orable's successive
husbands we should expect, and which should have preceded this
scene: Guillaume has won without a fight and the rest is mere
tidying up which the audience can enjoy with gusto, however badly
things seem to go for the hero.

The poet shows his versatility in this passage, as the arming of
Guïelin takes a much more conventional turn. His mail shirt and
helmet are both impervious to all attack. The former was forged by
Ysac de Barceloigne; the latter passed down from Aufar de
Babiloine (Cairo), the first king either of Orange or of Babiloine
itself (the text is ambiguous). Thus between them, allowing for the
habitual assimilation of Jews to Muslims in the *chansons de geste*,
they encompass the prestige of the Islamic world from west to east,
Barcelona clearly being considered part of 'pagan Spain' in *PO*, and
not as Guillaume's city as in *ChG*. His sword had a more chequered
career. Originally owned by Tornemont de Valsone, it was stolen
and bought by Tiebaut, who thought (the verb 'cuidier' used by the
poet implies his self-deception) he would win his son (presumably
Arragon) a crown with it. The line referring to his spear is the most
puzzling of all: 'L'espié li baille madame de Valronne' (*AB* l.983).

Does it imply that the spear had belonged to an Amazon, or is this merely the name of the lady-in-waiting, introduced belatedly to fill a rhyme? It is possible, of course, that we are simply dealing with a passage that has become hopelessly corrupt in transmission. The *B* family manuscripts omit the reference, and *C* falls back on the banal 'dont bien tranche la pointe' (l.902). However *D* offers 'L'espiet li done Brundenel de Valdonne' (l.830), which by its formulation confirms the name as that of the possessor of the spear, while the element '-donne' at the end of the name is probably to be equated with 'lady', confirming the original owner as an Amazon, and validating *A*'s reading. Just as the reader is getting used to the conventional timelessness of the epic arming motif, the narrator breaks the poetic spell to remind us that events are proceeding apace in the space-time continuum of the narrative. Gillebert's arming is left incomplete since

> Ainz qu'il eüst le bon trenchant espié,
> Felon paien orent tant esploitié
> Que les degrez en monterent a pié.
>
> (*AB* 993–95)

and we are thrown into the hurly-burly of an epic battle with shattering spears whose splinters fly high in the sky and sword blows that cut opponents in two. This breaking of epic expectations could well have struck a realistic chord with the audience of knights who knew that the enemy did not stand around whistling while you armed yourself. The poet achieves this, however, with far less undermining effect than the poet of *Le Couronnement de Louis* did when, at the end of an interminable *prière du plus grand péril* (*24*, *AB* ll.699–793), normally also considered to take place outside time and not interrupt the narrative continuum, he had Corsolt ask Guillaume 'A qui as tu si longement parlé?' (l.798).

This epic prayer or credo, the next motif I wish to consider, is usually uttered by the hero in times of extreme danger, or as a prelude to a particularly important battle; it is a well-established feature of *chansons de geste* (*67*). In true feudal fashion it constitutes a reciprocal contract with the Deity, as, following the recitation of the main elements in the story of salvation (from Creation, through several Old Testament prefigurations of the death and resurrection of Christ, to the Gospel story itself), it regularly concludes with a formula equivalent to 'as I believe this so You should save/help/protect me'. In fact such prayers are comparatively rare in the earlier poems of the cycle. *ChG* has none (although Vivien's 'Gethsemane' prayers follow a similar model), nor does *Le Charroi de Nîmes*. There is one brief one, spoken by Aimeri, in *Les Enfances Guillaume* (ll.410–14), but the major examples in the 'core' of the cycle are found in *Le Couronnement de Louis*: the one already cited which comes immediately prior to Guillaume's duel with Corsolt (*24*, *AB* ll.699–793), and one pronounced during the battle when he is narrowly missed by a javelin (*24*, *AB* ll.977–1029). Even though the two prayers in *Le Couronnement de Louis* come at an appropriate moment, when the hero has to fight a pagan enemy with truly diabolic overtones (*51*, pp.37–41), and are not repeated when the opponent is a Christian however fearsome, the poet seems to take them less than seriously as a literary motif. It is less clear, at least at first sight, what the attitude of the author of *PO* is. Redaction *AB* presents us with four such prayers, although in embryonic form (ll.499–509; 541–44; 783–90; 803–17). Not only do they offer a crescendo in terms of length and content but they steadily build up tension as the moment of true conflict approaches. In the first two one could not say that Guillaume is in any peril at all. His disguise as a Saracen messenger is still complete and the prayers are uttered in response to threats made more or less at random by Arragon. The last two do come at moments when there is real peril, when Guillaume's make-up is removed and when battle is imminent, although as yet the Christians have no weapons. Once Guillaume and his companions are armed these prayers vanish from the poem to be replaced by appeals to the solidarity of the clan, although usually in the inverted form of a lament over the absence of Guillaume's brothers and his fear that he will not see them again (*AB* ll.905–08; 1326–35; 1569–78). This clear division in approach would confirm distinct origins for the spying mission and the battle for Orange. If, as most critics do, we take the prayers seriously, we would have to conclude that in the first part of the poem there is a reliance on divine support which is abnormal in the Guillaume Cycle (*72*, 1, p.112), but in which the hero has his simple faith rewarded by escaping detection until in a position to take up at least improvised arms, and then being accorded a victory over an enemy vastly superior in numbers. To this extent the first 1,000 lines of the poem could be considered a vindication of Vivien's and Saint Bernard's views (see above, pp.35–37). The second part, in which Guillaume relies on human resources, would show him somewhat demeaned, as Guïelin has to call him to order, rather as he does in the 'Gui section' of *G1*, before a less than heroic Guillaume is prepared to put up a fight in a battle eventually won for him by his nephew. This ideological opposition is not as clear as it seems, however, and the comic and possibly parodic use of the prayer motif will be considered below (pp.108–10).

The replacement of the prayer motif by a variation on the lament in the second half of the poem introduces the last major epic motif exploited by the poet. The lament over a fallen warrior, or *planctus* (*135*), is one of the most widespread motifs in epic poetry, and, along with the eulogy of the chief or warrior may be seen as constitutive of the epic genre in general. There are two forms which are used in the Old French poems, one based on the Biblical and classical '*ubi sunt?*' rhetorical figure (which asks 'Where are the great ones of the past?'), used by Guibourc to question Guillaume about the warriors lost at l'Archamp (*ChG*, ll.2337–77) or by Charlemagne when surveying the fallen at Roncevaux (*17*, ll.2402–10). In *PO*, there is a very brief allusion to this type of lament when Bertrand questions Gillebert on his return to Nîmes (*AB* ll.1734–35). The other, more common type has a formulaic sequence beginning with an expression of regret that such promise has been cut short, giving a formal catalogue of the dead warrior's illustrious kin and/or deeds, depicting the particular hardships that the loss will impose on the speaker or his community, and finishing with an expression of personal grief, often amounting to a wish not to outlive the dead hero. This style of lament, as used by

Charlemagne in a specific lament over Roland (*17*, ll.2897–942), is the one which dominates the penultimate episode of *PO*. Using a device similar to the cinematic cut from scene to scene, which permits the use of dramatic irony, the poet takes us ahead of Gillebert as he returns to Nîmes after escaping from the secret tunnel and reveals Bertrand alone on the walls of the recently conquered town. There, in a protracted speech (*AB* ll.1671–1726), he laments the deaths of Guillaume and Guïelin. That he should not mention Gillebert, a stranger to the clan, is not surprising. What is more surprising is that he stresses Guillaume's folly in going secretly and on foot to Orange (*90*, p.209) rather than singing his uncle's praises in a sequence beginning 'mar fu'. Equally, even compared to the space Charlemagne devotes to the problems Roland's death will cause him (*17*, ll.2921–27), the insistence with which Bertrand anticipates his own slaughter at the hands of a carefully catalogued list of pagan kings and their vast forces (*AB* ll.1680–87) does tend, as Lachet suggests, to diminish the stature of both the speaker and the subject of his lament. This effect may actually be exaggerated by the use of a pair of *laisses similaires* to expound the motif at the hinge of which (*AB* ll.1703–04) Bertrand faints on what appear as purely conventional marble steps and has to be helped up by his barons. Indeed, the sharpness of the 'cut' in mid-*laisse* from Gillebert's announced arrival at Nîmes (*AB* l.1659) to Bertrand, in a scene which combines the 'view from the tower' (*97*) and a *raverdie* (*69*, pp.169–78) echoing the opening of the poem (*AB* ll.1660–66), may be calculated to jolt the audience considerably. However, just as Charlemagne gives the lie to his misgivings by going on to defeat Baligant, so Bertrand rapidly recovers from his despair and accomplishes the exploit attributed to him in at least part of the received tradition. What remains alien to the presuppositions which the audience would have about the motif and its use is that the lament is pronounced other than in the presence of the fallen hero, and on the mere suspicion of the subject's demise.

We should, however, bear in mind the different expectations aroused in the audience by, for instance, the mutual laments of

Lancelot and Guinevere, or Pyramus and Thisbé, over the supposed death of the loved one (*26*, ll.4197–396; *31*, ll.708–889), with the sense of tragic humanity which these episodes generate. In this light, allowing for the romance or lyric setting of the lament and its being properly addressed by a male to a male rather than to a female subject, the role of this motif, as of others we have considered in this chapter, may be to challenge the audience's expectations about the kind of literature they are receiving. The epic is beginning to live in an uncomfortable symbiosis with the 'courtly' genres.

An Essay in Style

One feature of *PO* observed by many critics and anchoring it firmly in the epic genre is the high density of its formulaic language, showing a much higher proportion of repeated elements than many older poems which sit less ambiguously in that tradition (*105*, pp.18–28; cf. *70*, p.23). This feature is variously taken as a sign of the oral origins of the text or as an indication of the art of the author (*70*, Chap.2, esp. pp.25–30 — which does not distinguish 'original' from extant versions — and 59–62; *80*, pp.42–43). It is, not surprisingly, seen as a major contributor to the poem's parodic effect (*90*, pp.132–46). Leaving aside the inherent circularity of arguments which relate formulæ to orality, what follows will concentrate on the ways in which the systematic exploitation of epic style reinforces the generic markers of the motifs studied in the last section, while creating tension with the courtly romance and lyric features examined in the next.

Much of the formulaic language which gives *PO* its quintessentially epic character, and which contributes also to the feeling that its *laisses* are hermetically isolated lyrico-narrative units in the manner of the *Roland* or *G1*, is found specifically at *laisse* boundaries. Rychner indicated in his early study of epic technique that an essential feature of the *laisse* as a musical structure, reinforcing its role as a poetic and narrative unit, is the autonomy of the first and last lines of the *laisse*, which he termed the *vers d'intonation* and the *vers de conclusion*, the former serving a deictic purpose (identifying and situating the character who will perform the action of the *laisse*), the latter encapsulating a comment on the action by a character or by the poet-narrator, or providing a résumé of what has passed (*115*, pp.69–74). A surprising feature of the composition of *PO* is the fixity of these *laisse* boundaries.

Of the seventy-two *laisses* constituting the *AB* redaction, thirty-seven have an opening line containing the name of Guillaume in one or other hemistich (cf. *104*, which considers similar material in relation to formulæ introducing direct speech). Of these, nineteen have as their first hemistich 'Or fu Guillelmes…' followed by either an adjectival phrase or an adverbial phrase of place in the second hemistich. Nor are these *laisses* scattered thinly and evenly through the poem; they are generally grouped in sequences by twos or threes:

Or fu Guillelmes en Orenge leanz (*AB* 450)

Or fu Guillelemes el palés sor la tor (*AB* 510)

Or fu Guillelmes el palés seignori (*AB* 545)

which set up a series of *laisses enchaînées* (the last two are strictly *bifurquées*, starting from the same point and developing the action in divergent directions), although the expectation aroused by the *vers d'intonation* is of *laisses parallèles*, in which the same static situation of the protagonist is presented from a shifting perspective (for discussions of these terms see *115*, Ch. IV). Here, however, the first of the series recounts the disguised Guillaume's initial contact with Arragon, his lie about being Tiebaut's messenger and escape from the captured Nîmes, and his *prière du plus grand péril* whispered in response to Arragon's threats; the second introduces an exchange with his nephew, Guïelin, in which the young man taunts his uncle about the amorous purpose of his visit to Orange, coming back through a loop to another *prière du plus grand péril* as Arragon finds an excuse to curse Guillaume when Orable is mentioned; the third moves right away from this material to describe the luxury of the meal served to the 'pagan messengers', which provokes in Guillaume the wish to conquer the town out of cupidity. The fixity of the epic writing is thus at odds with a continuous narrative line that can be represented as:

hero enters stronghold → hero reminded of mission → hero entertained to meal.

Interwoven with this is the motif of a duplicitous conversation between the hero and his enemy (but on two differing topics) with another convolution supplied by repeated prayers by the hero (two — rather pusillanimous, given that he is in no immediate danger — for his own safety; one for the support of an ally to expedite the conquest of the town for booty). It is therefore only at the level of motifs that there is any element of that lyric stasis which Pickens (*109*) has identified as an essential component of the poetics of the epic, but its contrast with the constant forward thrust of the narrative prevents us on this occasion from experiencing that sense of timelessness which is the essence of such moments in earlier *chansons*. The effect here is rather to highlight the rigidity of epic composition.

This rigidity of composition is a feature which Régnier (*5*, p.73) noticed. The habit of the *AB* redactor in particular of repeating formulæ verbatim, with only minor variations imposed by changing assonances, provides exactly that incantatory register so typical of the epic. Yet once again this rigidity is exploited to produce some incongruity by being set against a narrative context in which it is out of place. So when, in two successive laments over the boredom of 'garrison life' devoid of military encounters, Guillaume uses the same formula, albeit with considerable reorganisation for once:

> Et Dex confonde Sarrazins et Esclers
> Qui tant nos lessent dormir et reposer,
> *Quant par efforz n'ont passee la mer*
> (AB 63–65)

> Et Dex confonde Sarrazins et Persant
> *Quant mer ne passent par lor efforcement*
> (AB 97–98)

this establishes an expectation which is redefined to potentially comic effect on its third appearance providing only minimal variation in relation to the first use:

> Cuida que fust Sarrazin ou Escler
> *Qui par efforz eüst passee mer*
> (AB 145–46)

The humour hinges on the pun in *par efforz* which should mean 'with great effort' in this line but which carries with it the idea of 'in great numbers' established in the first two appearances of the formula. The audience is thus left with the bizarre perception of Guillaume mistaking one woebegone Christian fugitive for a whole pagan army largely because he is 'black' and dishevelled.

    A complex and somewhat disorienting example of this mode of composition is found in the account of the first battle between the three Franks and the Saracens once Guillaume has been unmasked by Salatré (*AB* ll.746–79), which extends over *laisses* 26–34 (*AB* ll.825–1069). The actual boundaries of this sequence are a little imprecise, but I shall exclude the *prières du plus grand péril* pronounced by Guillaume, the killing of Salatré and the opening of the sequence under discussion, since it has become totally garbled in the *AB* version, which as elsewhere attempts to maximise the presence of Guillaume in the text, to the detriment of Guïelin, who is given prominence in *C* and *D*. What one notices first about the rest of the sequence is that three *laisses* begin with an assertion that the companions suffer great anguish because they are trapped in Gloriëte (*AB* ll.899–901, 923–25, 1024–28); two of the *laisses* follow each other, but the third in the sequence is separated from its fellows by the arming of Guillaume, Guïelin and Gillebert and a renewed assault by the Saracens.

This arming of the heroes, starting with Guillaume, comes in the second of the pair of *laisses bifurquées* (29–30), the first of which offers one in a series of *laisses* in which, Guillaume having expressed despair over their position, Guïelin retorts that his uncle has a splendid opportunity to make love to Orable, which is what he came to do in the first place (see also *laisses* 17: Guillaume should ask to be taken to Orable, 43: Guillaume should ask Orable to save her lover 'par amours', 54: Guïelin rounds on them both urging them to make love). The use of such a recurrent motif, even if offering non-epic content, ties the passage and those with which it forms a chain into epic mode, imposing a manner of interpretation on the audience (*98*, pp.179–87; *80*, pp.305–25). Guillaume's despair seems to be justified at the start of *laisse* 30, however, since Orable's speech, which is the first main item, calls on the Franks to surrender. In this context her decision to give Guillaume her husband's arms is unmotivated in *AB*, as it is in *D*. *C* offers a more cogent link as Orable reports a vision predicting her conversion (ll.854–67), which provides religious, and hence psychological, motivation for the action. The arming itself follows strict epic patterns: hauberk, helmet, sword, shield and spear are provided to each in strict order (*AB* ll.944–57 and 968–84) but whereas the various items given to Guïelin are provided with an epic background (but subverted since, for instance, the sword was first stolen then sold, not won in battle, ll.976–79), those given to Guillaume are presented decoratively: the hauberk is gilded, the helmet studded with gems, the lance fitted with a pennon attached by five gold rivets. If this tends to give Guïelin more of a military presence, and Guillaume more of a decorative one, that would fit the older man's role as lover in this poem, but we should notice that the shield Orable gives Guillaume is fully described: a lion crowned or, suggesting sovereignty, within a bordure (tinctures unspecified). A strictly parallel link is also made between the pair in the swords provided: both are associated with Tiebaut and are presented in such a way as to indicate that power and heritable rights have passed from him and his son, Arragon, to Guillaume and his nephew

Guïelin, suggesting a relationship made explicit in *ChG* (ll. 1446–83).

The formal linking of these *laisse*s is reinforced by their actually also being *laisses enchaînées*, the *vers de conclusion* of each providing the basis of the *vers d'intonation* for the following:

> «Dex, dist Guillelmes, comme or sui bien armé!
> Por Deu vos pri que des autres pensez.»
>> (*AB* 958–59)

> Quant Guïelin vit adoubé son oncle
> Cort en la chanbre a la dame seconde...
>> (*AB* 960–61)

> Bien fu armez, et Gilleberz adonques.
> Huimés avra Glorïete chalonge.
>> (*AB* 985–86)

> Bien fu armez Guillelmes et se niés
> Et Gillebert, dont sont joiant et lié.
>> (*AB* 987–88)

The close parallel between quotations 1, 3 and 4 suggests the atemporal, lyric privileging of the moment of arming at the expense of narrative continuity. Moreover, the lyric stasis highlights the 'knighting of Guillaume and Gui' (made explicit in *D*, see pp. 53–54) and reduces the equipping of Gillebert to a single hemistich (985b). The artificiality of the epic proceeding is then revealed as the arming of Gillebert is described (*AB* ll. 989–92; redactions *C* and *D* do not have this sequence) and interrupted before he can receive his spear with its pennon by the eruption into the room of the host of Saracen warriors (*AB* ll. 993–95). This in turn introduces a sequence of '*vers parallèles*' (being the abbreviated equivalent of *laisses parallèles*) in which the three Franks in turn kill a named enemy (*AB* ll. 996–1012). The climax of the sequence is the driving of the enemy from the tower, the barring of the doors and the raising of the drawbridge. This apparently logical epic narrative is then interrupted again by the return of the formulaic line 'Or fu Guillelmes dolant et correços' (*AB* l.1024) which suppresses narrative chronology and restores the situation as it was some hundred lines earlier, complete with Guillaume's despair, countered this time by a martial assertion from Guïelin that he at least will sell his life dearly (*AB* ll.1030–35).

The circularity of this episode in *AB* is further accentuated by the repeated clearing of the tower. This first happens before the heroes are armed, culminating then as in the later sequence with the statement that fourteen Saracens were killed (l.854; cf. l.1016; also ll.1039 and 1066), and ending with the doors being barred and the drawbridge raised (ll.856–58). The closing sequence of *laisse* 26 then introduces an appeal to God from the narrator ('Or en penst Dex, qui en croiz fu pené!', *AB* l.859) since the heroes are in a perilous plight as the Saracens press their attack. This is closely echoed in *laisse* 32 ('Or en penst Dex qui tot a a jugier! / Voit l'Arragon, le sens cuide changier', *AB* ll.1022–23), although the last line allows a new link, not to the next *laisse* which portrays Guillaume's distress, but to the end of *laisse* 34 and the start of *laisse* 35, which constitute a pair of *laisses enchaînées* reflecting Arragon's rage at the massacre of his warriors.

This complex series of duplications and interlacings gives a very emphatic stress to the passage as epic discourse, with formulæ supporting motifs, at the expense of narrative logic. The feeling that this engenders that we are dealing with an exercise in pure style, at least in the *AB* redaction, is reinforced by the differences apparent in the other redactions. While *C* maintains enough of the circularity of *AB*'s writing to suggest that some of it derives from the archetype of the families *A*, *B* and *C* (cf. the stemma: *5*, p.28) the impact is firstly reduced by the reduction of the number of *laisses* (*AB laisses* 26–29 = *C laisse* 26) with a consequent loss of repetitive *vers d'intonation*, then further alleviated by the suppression of Guillaume's voice on many occasions, his speeches being attributed to Guïelin (or on one occasion Gillebert). In this version narrative logic is restored while epic impact is lost. Redaction *D*, which

derives independently from the cyclic archetype (*5*, p.28), while also
expanding the role of Guïelin at the expense of his uncle, like *C*
suppresses much of the formulaic circularity, not by amalgamating
*laisse*s, but by omitting them. Notably the *vers d'intonation*
referring to Guillaume's distress comes only twice (*D* ll.765, 787)
before the Franks are armed, and is then reintroduced only at ll.941,
949 and 1016, where they are taken by surprise through the
underground passage and thrown into the dungeon. The formula is
not used in comparable passages of *AB* or *C*. What survives in all
three redactions is the double closing of the doors and raising of the
drawbridge, suggesting that this particular narrative illogicality
belongs to the cyclic archetype. It also seems likely from a
comparison of the three versions that, for all the problems it
otherwise raises, *D* in its 'epic linearity' reflects most faithfully the
presentation of the story in that version; the original of *AB* + *C* will
then have exaggerated the epic stylistic markers of the text, possibly
for comic or parodic purposes (*90*, pp.14–48; cf. below, pp.108ff.),
which *C* then reduced to assimilate the text more closely to romance
mode.

The Courtly Dimension

Although, as we have seen, the surface features of *PO*, and some of
its underlying narrative motifs, belong firmly to epic poetry, many
other elements, including some of the most important structural
ones, derive from courtly models (*90*, pp.151–58). The notion of the
history of twelfth-century French literature as a simple linear
evolution from epic to romance, with the 'newer' genre then
exerting an influence on the later, 'decadent' *chansons de geste*, is
no longer generally held to be tenable. The first generation of
romances (from ca 1150) were strongly influenced by the epic, as
were the early romances of Chrétien de Troyes, while the Arthurian
prose romances and non-Arthurian 'social' romances of the
thirteenth century give renewed prominence to epic features. Nor
was the romance immune from the earlier manifestation of courtly
culture, the lyricism of *grant chant courtois* transmitted from the

South (*136*, pp.286–321, 380–404). Likewise the epic, which had inherently lyric qualities in its poetic structures (*94*; *109*) was not averse to absorbing elements of the newer lyricism to revitalise its own modes of expression. Thus at the artistically important turning-point of 1200 (*119*) we find these modes co-existing in loose constellations and available for exploitation in varied combinations by increasingly sophisticated writers in all genres.

No aspect of the writing of the extant cyclic *PO* is immune from this atmosphere, but it is particularly apparent in the presentation of Orable in her role as 'Enamoured Muslim Princess' (*126*). This character type seems to have been invented in the 1170s and may have been used first in *Fierabras* (*52*, p.11). One important feature of the Saracen princess for writers of the time was her very exoticism in comparison to the French, Christian, lady. Like the equally exotic (non-aristocratic) shepherdess of the *pastourelle*, she has licence to exhibit a sensuality not permitted to her 'courtly' sister, and is seen as available for a more direct approach. Orable shows all of these characteristics from the moment we are introduced to her.

Passing over Gillebert's description of her, which I shall consider when examining the presentation of Guillaume's reactions, we next see Orable through the eyes of her stepson, Arragon. His role as surrogate for Tiebaut extends to presenting a 'moralist's' picture of the Queen as *mal mariée* (*90*, pp.158–62). This figure, who is known from pre-courtly northern lyric, troubadour *chanson* and narrative texts such as *Guigemar* and *Yonec* by Marie de France, is a young, aristocratic lady married to an unsuitable husband, who may beat her, and certainly keeps her strictly enclosed out of jealousy. The man may be unsuitable by birth (he is a bourgeois or a peasant) or simply be old. His essential role is to treat his wife as property and to repress her natural yearnings for love, which can only be satisfied by her free acceptance of a reciprocal relationship with a young *bacheler*. Tiebaut's unsuitability is predicated by his being a husband imposed by Orable's brothers (who are the communal head of the family in most of the tradition, cf. *100*), and on his being a pagan capable of engendering a son like Arragon:

> «Li ainznez filz a Tiebaut l'Esclavon;
> Granz est et gros et parcreüs et lons,
> Lee la teste et enbarré le front
> Et granz les ongles et agües en son;
> N'a tel tirant soz la chape del mont,
> Noz crestïens nos ocit et confont.»
>
> (*AB* 230–35)

This physical presentation through the eyes of Gillebert (which in the last two lines appears to conflate father and son) is not replicated when the narrator introduces Arragon in person. However, the stance the Saracen adopts, criticising his father's folly in marrying a young woman (*AB* ll.619–21; 628–29) and also criticising her for blatantly carrying on her affairs ('ses drüeries', *AB* l.623) with *bachelers* like Sorbant de Venice, a champion of tournaments (*AB* ll.624–26), assigns to Arragon the role of *losengier* (moralising scandal-monger and enemy of lovers) from the courtly tradition, coupled with that of clerkly misogynist and jealous guardian of the *mal mariée*. The moralising and misogynist aspects are accentuated in *C* which attributes to Arragon the more explicit commentary

> «Par Mahommet que je aour et prie,
> Faus est viel homme qui prent jovene mescine,
> Qu'ele velt estre acolee et baisie
> Et viels hom n'a cure de tele vie;
> Tost en est coz et honis par folie.»
>
> (*C* 593–97)

while *D*, taking account of *Les Enfances Guillaume*, adds 'dan Guillelme de France la garnie' (l.501) to the list of Orable's lovers in a context that deflects criticism away from Orable and focuses attention on Guillaume as the adversary.

In the light of this it is no surprise that when we first see Orable it is in a situation at once courtly and seductive. The lady herself has the conventional colouring of heroines of romance: 'Ele est plus blanche que la noif qui resplent / Et plus vermeille que la rose flerant' (*AB* ll.666–67), a combination that dates back to Antiquity. In the twelfth century we find the figure applied metonymically to Briseïda's cloak, when she first meets Troïlus in the *Roman de Troie* of Benoist de Sainte Maure (*8*, ll.13344–45) and then to the young woman Polyxena (*8*, ll.26450–51) when she appears as an object of pity to the people when she is condemned to death. It is regularly used as an element of the description of his heroines by Chrétien de Troyes, who uses it symbolically to represent the absent Blancheflor in the scene in *Le Conte du Graal* in which Perceval contemplates drops of blood lying on snow inducing a lover's reverie (*28*, ll.4164–93). This type of description enters the epic only once it has absorbed the lessons of romance writing, as in *Maugis d'Aigremont* (an early thirteenth-century epic) in which the fairy Oriande is described now as being 'à la fresche color' (*29*, l.560), now as 'la bele à la color rosine' (*29*, l.1176). If the scent of spices has aphrodisiac implications, and the fashionable figure-hugging dress Orable is wearing may incline us to view the scene as one of sensual delights, the image of Rosiane fanning Orable with a solid silver fan removes us into a more ritual atmosphere (*52*, p.4, note 12; *90*, pp.70–71). The fan also belongs to that level of 'realistic' exoticism which marks much of the description of Orable's apartment with its silver filigree windows, marble pillars and inlaid benches (*AB* ll.645–50; 673–74), all of which create a heightened atmosphere of Islamic palace architecture (as in the twelfth-century Alcazar at Seville, *134*, pp.151–58). The Oriental reference also survives in the very name of Orable's tower: 'gloriete' being the French rendering of the Arabic *al-'aziz* ('the glorious') found in an inscription on the garden-palace in Palermo and thus applied to the raised gazebo usually placed at the heart of a garden both to catch any breezes available and to give a perspective over the formal layout of the garden (*79*, pp.39, 44; *88*, pp.324–29; for other interpretations of the name cf. *72*, 2, pp.293–94; *96*, pp.32–40). The multi-layered references in the description are brought together in the tree found in the chamber:

> A une part de la chambre leanz
> Avoit un pin par tel esperiment. . .
> Longue est la branche et la fueille en est grant;
> La flor qu'en ist par est si avenant,
> Blanche est et inde et si est vermeillant.
>
> (*AB* 651–56)

This tree, under which Guillaume and Orable sit to talk, is a synthesis of the whole scene: its colours include those associated with the lady herself, it is both an evergreen and a broadleaf tree, evidently in flower, and although it apparently grows indoors it is the noble 'pillar of the universe' (*88*, pp.306–18) under which Charlemagne sits to deliberate in the *Roland* (*17*, ll.114–16). In this way Moorish or Saracen exoticism is linked with Classical and romance themes and possibly echoes of the Bible (the tree recalls both Eden and the New Jerusalem) to generate a global image of Orable's tower as a paradise to be conquered or regained.

It is clear, even in *AB*, which most completely confuses Glorïete and Orange, that there is a distinction between Orable's realm and that of the diabolic pagans without. Orable is no *mal mariée* imprisoned in her tower, but has power to command in her own realm: she denies Arragon access to her tower (*AB* ll.1238–43; *D* l.970 refers to her 'court'), demanding that the prisoners be handed over to her to await Tiebaut's return and not executed out of hand (*AB* ll.1245–46: the reading 'ta prison' of the *A* manuscripts is presumably an error, as 'ma chartre' (*D* l.963) is supported by B^2 'ma prison', cf. *5*, p.147). Equally, despite the slanders of the pagan spy who claims to have seen Orable and Guillaume hugging, kissing and behaving intimately (*AB* ll.1478–81), she has none of the forwardness of the Saracen princess as found in other epics, nor of the heroines of some romances. When she enters Guillaume's prison it is not, like Esclarmonde in *Huon de Bordeaux* (*16*, ll.5881–88) or the seneschal's wife in Chrétien's *Lancelot* (*26*, ll.5476–81), to offer herself blatantly to the hero as the price of his release. Likewise her dress with its side lacings may at first blush evoke memories of the fairy in Marie de France's *Lanval* 'vestue en itel guise / De chainse blanc et de chemise / Que tuit li costé li pareient' (ll.559–61: *23*, p.89), who uses her sexuality as a reward for Lanval and as a weapon against Arthur and his barons, but Orable, by contrast, remains determinedly chaste with Guillaume, indulging in nothing more erotic than a game of chess with him, in company with Guïelin (*AB* ll.1495–97). Her sighs on hearing of Guillaume's military prowess may indicate an instant falling in love, but all she asks of the hero is a guarantee of marriage in return for conversion (*AB* ll.1374–78). On those terms she will release them so that they can hold the tower until Louis and the Narbonnais arrive to relieve them (*AB* ll.136070).

Orable's falling in love with the absent hero on the strength of a report is a well known motif in twelfth-century literature. The fairy in *Lanval* tells the hero that she has come from her own land specifically to seek him out (ll.110–12: *23*, p.75), although her knowledge of him is presumably supernatural. On the other hand it is purely on account of a report made by a human agent that Floripas in *Fierabras* falls in love with Gui de Bourgogne (*12*, ll.2056ff.) and that Laudine insists on sending for Yvain (*27*, ll.1545–1880). It is also notable that in the latter case, as in that of *PO*, the object of the report is actually present in the castle, allowing both poets to exploit the humorous possibilities of the situation.

This is a narrative variation on the lyric theme of *amor de lonh* (love from afar or of the distant, unattainable object). The theme seems to be as old as troubadour poetry itself since Guillaume IX (died 1121) already satirises it in his poem 'Faray un vers de dreit nien' ('I shall compose a poem on nothing at all'), but it was given its definitive form in the songs of Jaufre Rudel (died 1148/50), in which the yearnings of human love are overlaid with a mysticism blended of love of God (and/or the Virgin) and a nostalgia for the holy places. Whether Jaufre's enigmatic poem 'Lanquan li jorn son lonc en may' ('When the days are long in May') was intended by this means to ennoble human love or to give a human dimension to divine love is an insoluble conundrum. At all events the use of the device of positing physical separation to symbolise the spiritual, emotional or moral gulf between the poet and his lady soon became a commonplace of the courtly lyric. Gace Brulé uses it, blended with the motif of the 'Spring Opening' in a poem which has as its first stanza:

> Les oiseillons de mon païs
>   Ai oïs en Bretaigne.
> A lor chant m'est il bien avis
>   Qu'en la douce Champaigne
>   Les oï jadis,
>   Se n'i ai mespris.
> Il m'ont en si dolz panser mis
> K'a chanson faire me sui pris
>   Tant que je parataigne
> Ce qu'amors m'a lonc tens promis.
>
>   (*19*, p.61)

It is precisely this same blend of *raverdie* and *amor de lonh* that strikes down Guillaume at the beginning of *PO*. The mixture of Spring, identified by the items 'May', 'flowers', 'bubbling brooks' and 'birdsong' (*AB* ll.39–43; 50–51), and the epic motif of the view from the tower, has already filled him with romantically nostalgic yearnings, as he misses the merry life of the French court he has left (*AB* ll.52–53) and particularly *jongleurs* and young women (*AB* ll.56–57). The lyric nature of his longing is emphasised by its being repeated in a pair of *laisses similaires* (3 and 4). However, the reader/hearer is disoriented by the motif's reaching its climax on each occasion with a reference to the distressing absence of pagans who are refusing to fight (*AB* ll.63–69; 97–100). The courtly motif is thus temporarily subverted by the expression of a military nostalgia akin to that expressed by Bertran de Born (see above, p.37). The arrival of Gillebert, fresh from his prison in Orange, soon sets matters to rights, however, as his report on the excellence of the city, and especially on the beauty of its queen, is so

compulsive for the hero that love soon has total control of his heart.
There is a steady crescendo in the poet's presentation of
Guillaume's state, as at first he places desire for the town as a prize
on a par with conquering Orable: 'Ja ne quier mes lance n'escu
porter / Se ge nen ai la dame et la cité' (*AB* ll.265–66); this soon
gives way to ever more insistent descriptions of the symptoms of
love (*AB* ll.283–92; 351–60) culminating in a statement which
defies our sense of chronology by its appeal to standard formulæ:

> «La seue amor m'a si fort jostisié
> Ne puis dormir par nuit ne someiller
> Ne si ne puis ne boivre ne mengier
> Ne porter armes ne monter sor destrier
> N'aler a messe ne entrer en moustier.»
> (*AB* 371–75)

Now, while we might be tempted to interpret these statements
'realistically' as engaging the future, their formulaic expression
relates them to the depiction of symptoms currently suffered by the
lover. The content of the lines mixes chivalric, possibly epic,
concerns (fighting, bearing arms) with lyric ones, and also throws in
abeyance Guillaume's devotion to his religion. Everything 'freezes'
in the timeless moment of pure lyricism, as it does in those
moments of heightened experience in the epic which also relate to
the lyric experience.

The use of this motif brings into sharp relief the way *PO*
exploits generic intertextuality (cf. *58*, Ch. I). It cannot be appreciated as epic or romance alone. The story of the capture of the town,
and of the finding of a wife for the hero, is carried on using
narrative elements and the poetic means of the *chansons de geste*.
However, the underlying diegetic structure, presupposing a lack (or
in this case a number of lacks) in the hero made good as a result of
his quest, belongs firmly to the folk-tale-derived romance model
(*65*, pp.371–72: he not only conquers the town and finds and
marries his love, but reinstates court life in all its glory — '.viii.
jorz durerent [les noces] a joie et a barné; / Assez i ot harpeor et

jugler', *AB* ll.1882–83 — and returns to church, having gained a convert to his religion, *AB* ll.1863–76). As a result the poem can only be appreciated not as a hybrid, and not as one genre commenting on the other, as Lachet would have it (*90*), but as a reflexion on the literary kinds prevalent at the end of the twelfth century.

3. Evolutions

Developing Characters

The links between *ChG* and *PO* are not merely those that may be expected in texts belonging or related to the same cycle. They have not only many themes but also many characters in common, and, pertinently, treat those characters in a complementary fashion as part of their poetico-fictive world. The question of the evolution of the treatment of these themes and characters is a complex one, since the distance between the poems is not a simple matter of chronology as we move from one end of the twelfth century to the other. Both songs evolved with the century and the presentation of the main actors in each story presupposes a history of changes in cultural attitudes and perceptions providing a multi-layered subtext to the surviving versions.

One startling feature of both poems compared to other epics, whether these belong to the Guillaume Cycle or not, is the displacement of enemy and hero alike. In many poems it may be debatable whether this or that character is the hero or the principal enemy, but nowhere do we find the vacuum where these characters ought to be, which is evident in both *ChG* and *PO*. This absence is a physical one as far as the enemy is concerned, and essentially a moral one in the case of the hero.

What is most striking about Guillaume is that it is when he is physically absent, during the first 900 lines of *G1*, that his moral authority is at its highest (see above, pp.26–31). Even during the later episodes of *ChG*, when he is present on the battlefield, he fails to dominate it. Not only is his victory over Desramé, as established by the narrator in the poem's prologue (ll.2–5), taken from him to be attributed to Gui, but in no episode is Guillaume portrayed in the elementary epic situation of despatching a significant enemy in single combat (with or without the addition of an epic blow with sword or lance). His only part in the Girard-Guischard episode is to offer consolation to the dying warriors. It is true that he leads 30,000 knights to the field (of whom significantly only half are fully equipped and ready for battle, ll.1098–1101), but once there he is swallowed into the mass of his men, emerging briefly to drive off equally anonymous enemies from around the bodies of his nephews (ll.1144 and 1184). His only other action is to pull a javelin from Guischard's body and use it to kill his assailant (ll.1222–24). While this final action may be considered a suitably epic riposte, reminiscent of Oliver's last act at Roncevaux (*17*, ll.1940–64), the contrasts between the two are very stark. Oliver had been attacked by the 'algaliphe' (a considerable opponent) whom he despatches with an epic blow of his sword, Hauteclere, after which he pronounces a suitable *gab* over his fallen foe; Guillaume makes do with returning the throwing spear of an unnamed opponent, in a manner which leaves open the possibility that for the only time in Old French epic the hero resorts to the unworthy tactic of killing an enemy at a distance. Even the poet's statement that the blow was delivered 'par grant vertu' (l.1224) is undermined by its being immediately followed by the repeated assertion that the hero does not run away, but merely leaves the field.

In the Gui episode, once Gui has gone for refreshment, his uncle is quickly reduced to a state of desperation by anonymous enemies, and, indeed, is totally passive as a warrior until his abortive duel with Desramé which closes *G1*. The disjunction between telling, whether by the poet in the 'prologue' or by other characters reporting on the hero's past exploits, and showing could not be greater. Taken with the defection of Tedbalt de Burges following his heroic boasts and the absence of any assurance of salvation to validate Vivien's sacrifice, it is hard to escape the conclusion that *G1* is an ironic meditation on the nature of heroism (*114*, pp.17–18).

Although *G2* does not share this bleak point of view, it is notable that Guillaume's martial role steadily diminishes as that part of the song proceeds. His duel with Alderufe, at the beginning of *G2*, occupies 119 lines (ll.2091–209), constituting the longest single episode of individual combat in the poem. This is followed up by his rescuing Christian prisoners (captured at Tours) before the gates of Orange (ll.2259–306). At this point it seems that normal heroic activity is being resumed, but that is an illusion. In the former episode Guillaume's position is undermined from the start by Alderufe's cataloguing (in true epic fashion) all the heroes Guillaume *cannot* be (including himself). Guillaume's bemused reply, 'Par ma fei... un de cels devoie estre' (l.2102), not only reveals the humorous illogicality of the pagan's assertions, but underscores the negative application of the epic motif of evoking a list of illustrious heroes before battle by reminding us that all the Aymerides participating in the battle are either dead or captured, except Guillaume. Moreover, more space is devoted by the poet to the death of the horse, Balçan, to Guillaume's laments over him and to those of Alderufe over the loss of his horse, Florescele, than to the duel. It is to put an abrupt end to these complaints that, in a movement reflecting Gui's finishing off of Desramé in *G1*, Guillaume finally decapitates Alderufe as he lies helpless on the ground with a severed leg.

In the latter episode Guillaume's heroism is further diminished by his wearing pagan armour, taken from the man he has just killed as a disguise to facilitate his escape from l'Archamp. Although not explicitly described at the time he kills Alderufe, his taking the pagan's armour is presupposed by the gatekeeper's statement at Orange (l.2232) and by the reactions of the pagans who assume Guillaume is Alderufe (ll.2277–78). As a result he meets minimal resistance. The hollowness already perceptible at the core of traditional heroism even in *G2* is emphasised by Guibourc's refusal to accept what her husband has done as proof of identity because 'plusurs homes se resemblent assez / de vasselage et de nobilitez' (ll.2313–14). This bizarre assertion, which runs counter to all epic conventions concerning the unique status of the hero, marks the end of the movement undermining the notion of individual heroism which began with Alderufe's refusal to recognise

Guillaume. Order is temporarily restored when Guillaume reveals the lump on his injured nose, received in the battle against Tedbalt l'Esturman previously recalled by Vivien and now evoked by Guibourc (ll.666–75 and 2309–12).

This physical mark of established heroic credentials abolishes the suppression of identity presupposed in the motif of the disguise (*117*, pp.343–44). We find a similar exploitation of this motif in *PO*, in which Guillaume's adoption of pagan dress, and staining of his face with herbs, seems to negate his heroic persona. While he may boast to himself that, provided Bertrand were there with 20,000 iron-clad Franks (*AB* l.566) he would himself kill eighty pagans (*AB* l.568), his reactions to threats made by Arragon against a Guillaume supposed to be many miles away is to offer prayers *du plus grand péril*, which can at best be seen as a melodramatic trick on the part of the narrator to induce a sympathetic *frisson* of fear in the audience. It does imply an uncharacteristic loss of confidence on the part of the hero in his capacities as a trickster. In this poem also it is his nose, almost a metonymic encapsulation of his career and personality, which, according to Bertrand (*AB* l.338), will reveal his uncle's true identity to the pagans, and it is only when Salatré wipes off his disguise that Guillaume recovers enough heroic energy to take on the assembled pagans of Orange. Significantly, when Salatré throws a cloak at Guillaume (*AB* ll.775–79) — or the contents of a cup at Gui (*C* ll.746–50) — and strikes him in the face, his nose is specifically mentioned, so that, although it is ostensibly his white skin that gives him away, the disfigurement which is the visible symbol of his heroic career seems to be what really betrays him. Conversely, the other symbol of Guillaume's heroic energy, his laugh, mentioned by Bertrand along with his nose, is not a feature of *PO* (*90*, p.171), and, most importantly, it is not represented in what may be considered as its classic formulation, found so frequently in *Le Charroi de Nîmes*, 's'en a un ris gité' (*110*; *111*).

It is by comparison with *Le Charroi de Nîmes* and *Aliscans* that we can most fully appreciate the vacuum left in *G2* and *PO* by this suppression of the hero's persona. In both of these other poems

Guillaume also adopts disguises comparable to those adopted in our texts, and for similar purposes. When in *Le Charroi de Nîmes* he disguises himself as an English merchant adopting the name Tiacre de Cantorbire, the disguise adds to his epic zest. Not only does he invent a suitably heroic career for himself as an international trader (*20*, ll.1189–1202), but when Otran, one of the 'twin' pagan kings of Nîmes, is reminded of the hero by the lump on 'Tiacre's' nose and threatens the supposedly absent Guillaume with ignominious death, the riposte is an exuberantly improvised account of how the lump was acquired,

> «Quant je fui juesnes, meschins et bachelers,
> Si deving lerres merveilleus por embler
> Et engingnierres ...
> Si m'en repristrent li juesne bacheler
> Et marcheant cui ge avoie enblé;
> A lor coteaus me coperent le nes ...»
> (*20*, 1234–40)

The contrast between this burlesque, full of vital energy, of the story of his heroic wound and the hollow figure vanquished by love in *PO*, or the warrior worn out by age and responsibility who presides over most of *ChG*, could not be greater.

In an episode of *Aliscans* much more closely parallel to the one in *G2*, Guillaume disguises himself as a pagan to escape from an initial débâcle to find reinforcements which will permit the avenging of Vivien. As in *ChG* he takes arms from the defeated Aerofle to aid his removal from the battlefield, and the disguise helps him twice: once when he meets Baudus and a group of Aerofle's relatives, once when he has to rescue Christian prisoners to prove his identity to Guibourc at Orange. In the first instance he improvises a speech in 'Saracen' (one of several languages Guillaume speaks in *Aliscans* as he does in *PO*) in which he boldly claims to have killed 'Guillaume' and to be on his way to hand Orable back to her legitimate husband, Tiebaut (*7*, ll.1785–99). On the second occasion his borrowed arms help him to defeat a small troop of Saracens and gain quick entry to Orange (to avoid the 20,000 Saracens pursuing him), but in circumstances that remain heroic. Guibourc stresses the difficulty of identifying people by their voice (7, l.2055) rather than suggesting that a hero cannot be known by his actions. Indeed, her insistence that the real Guillaume would not be afraid even of the vast horde of Saracens currently pursuing him adds to the facile but compelling sense of heroic exaggeration in the whole episode, which reaches a climax when Guillaume, still speaking 'Pagan', forces some of his pursuers to give up their horses as ransom for having been absent from l'Archamp (7, ll.2122–35) while Guibourc, astounded at his temerity and fearful for his safety, prays to the Virgin for him and begs him to come within the safety of the walls of Orange (7, ll.2136–47). This, taken with the cry from the Saracen chorus when Guillaume's red silks and ermine betray him:

> «Par Mahomet, n'en irez pas einsint;
> Ne vos i vaut barat un romaisin!
> Ahi, Guillelmes, fel traître mastin,
> Tant vos savez de barat et d'engin!»
>   (7, 1807–10)

provoking a defiantly rude retort from the hero, gives a sense that poet and character relish equally the trickery and the heroism. Again we are far removed in atmosphere from the forlorn figure cut by the hero in *ChG*, and from the equivocal character, who trembles and prays before Arragon in *PO*.

The physical absence of the enemy commander in each poem has a different effect, though one that is equally disturbing of our expectations of epic. Whether we are concerned with a battle between Christians and pagans (as in the *Roland* or *Aspremont*) or with a feudal conflict between the king and a vassal (as in *Girart de Vienne* or *La Chevalerie Ogier de Danemarche*), the poem traditionally offers a parallel presentation of protagonist and antagonist, including verbal exchanges (direct or mediated) as a prelude to physical combat and the climactic confrontation of the two commanders on the battlefield. This schema is subverted in both *ChG* and *PO*.

The subversion is actually double in *ChG* because of the way the extant poem has been constructed. Although the presence of Desramé in France is announced from the beginning of the poem, this is done through a fugitive messenger who has escaped from a disaster inflicted by an enemy who remains faceless, a status he maintains through virtually the whole of *G1* together with his army, and even more obviously so through *G2,* since he has died at the end of *G1* and even his surrogate, Alderufe, is killed before the definitive battle is fought. Desramé's 'survival' into *G2* is as a character with a totally different status from that which he has at the beginning of the poem: instead of being a threatening enemy he is transformed into the father of Guibourc and Rainoart (*100*) and the means of endowing them with a glittering lineage, parallel and equal to that of the Aymerides. Desramé's absence from *G2* cannot be explained by the poet's reluctance to have relatives in conflict, as Rainoart confronts and kills other members of his own clan (ll.3273ff.; 3548), while in the equivalent part of *Aliscans* Desramé is actively presented as the enemy commander, who flees in the last undestroyed boat to live and fight another day. The immediate effect of the double displacement of the enemy commander in *ChG* is to enhance the role of the Saracens in *G1* as representatives of a universally intangible evil; in *G2* the uncoupling of the prestige of the 'fort rei Deramé' (l.2825) from the host of increasingly monstrous pagans slaughtered with gay abandon by Rainoart prevents ambiguity arising over the status of his children in their new community, while contributing to the lightening of the atmosphere already noted in *G2* (see above, pp.49–50).

The absence of Tiebaut in *PO* is very different in effect, as for most of the poem it is not noticeable, since he is replaced by his son Arragon. Though Tiebaut is mentioned frequently at the start of the poem, his name recurs in formulæ associating him with Orable or Arragon, which actually empty the reference of any serious content:

[Guillaume] Prist a moillier Orable la roïne ...

> Et si fu feme le roi Tiebaut d'Afrique
>> (*AB*, 25–27; cf. 34–35, 252–53, 275–76)
> Et Arragons, uns riches rois Aufaigne,
> Filz est Tiebaut de la terre d'Espaigne
>> (*AB* 200–01; cf. 229–30)

While these lines appear to give Tiebaut status (as husband and father), this is negated by his being incorporated into descriptions of other characters, a textual subordination which suppresses his autonomy and authority as the hero's adversary. His absence is so far axiomatic in the poem that when Guillaume and his party arrive at the gates of Orange they can pose as messengers sent by Tiebaut from Africa. The only time when his name is mentioned in a context suggesting serious threat comes when Bertrand is trying to dissuade his uncle from attempting his reconnaissance of Orange:

> «…cele gent sarrazine,
> Connoistront vos a la boce et au rire…
> Mengeront vos sanz pain et sanz farine…
> Giteront vos en lor chartre perrine,
> N'en istroiz mes a nul jor de vo vie
> Tant que venra le roi Tiebauz d'Aufrique
> Et Desramez et Gollïas de Bile,
> A lor talant feront de vos justise.»
>> (*AB* 337–47)

Even here the context, mixed of comic hyperbole ('they'll eat you alive') and conventional listing, reduces Tiebaut to the rank of mere cipher.

Now this is a startling innovation compared with the established traditions concerning the capture of Orange (see below, pp.115–17). As represented in Vivien's message to Guillaume in *G1* (ll.669–76), in Guibourc's suspicious challenge to her husband in *G2* (ll.2309–12), as well as in much of the later cyclic tradition, Guillaume came into direct conflict with Tiebaut over Orange. His textual demotion constitutes part of the generic shifts which the

reviser of the extant version has imposed on the inherited poem
(*76*), shifts first signalled in *Le Charroi de Nimes*, when Louis
objects (in terms similar to those employed by Bertrand in *PO*) to
Guillaume's expedition to the south:

> «Le roi Tiebaut i doit l'en coroner;
> Prise a Orable, la seror l'amiré...
> Por ce crien ge, se entr'eus vos metez,
> Que cele terre ne puissiez aquiter.»
> (*20*, 521–26)

Again we must note that Tiebaut comes at the end of a long list of
pagan kings (including Desramé, Golias and Arroganz) who will
resist the invasion, but the effect of these lines is to produce a
crescendo in which Louis foresees Guillaume's interposing himself
between the new bride and groom as the likely cause of disaster.
While this maintains the tradition of personal combat between
Orable's first and second husbands, it does indicate that the poetic
fiction is emphasising the marital conflict over habitual epic
concerns. In the courtly tradition, and particularly in the sub-
tradition of the *mal mariée* which dominates in *PO*, the husband,
while posing a latent threat to the lover and his lady, is literally a
non-entity, an absence in the text less effective than the *losengiers*
in keeping the lovers apart. The latter role is taken by Arragon, who
accuses his step-mother of multiple affairs (*drüeries*) in her tower of
Gloriete, preferring young *bachelers* to her elderly husband (*AB*
ll.619–29), and who reports to Tiebaut that Guillaume wants to take
his wife as *amie* (*AB* l.1285). Although Tiebaut reacts immediately,
and with a laugh that could be considered heroic (*AB* l.1297), the
laisse ends with the statement from the narrator that before his fleet
can reach Orange Tiebaut will have lost his city and his wife (*AB*
ll.1323–24). In fact the loss has already occurred in the moral
conflict which Guillaume won when Orable gave him Tiebaut's
armour, kept symbolically hanging in a cupboard in her chamber
figuring the hollowness of the husband's position, and his sword,
whose equally usurped role as commanding Phallus is emphasised

by the fact that Tiebaut would share it with no man, not even his own son (*AB* ll.949–53). The final indication of the adversary's nullity is that Orable takes responsibility for transferring herself from pagan to Christian husband. Such valorisation of the female will is extremely rare in medieval literature (*59*, pp.241–43), and occurs in comparable examples of courtly narrative only where the husband is a tyrant of the most despicable kind, as in the *lais* of *Guigemar* and *Yonec* by Marie de France (*23*, pp.12–13, 102–03).

The characters who provide stability in these two poems are Guillaume's nephews, Gui and Bertrand, and above all his wife, Orable-Guibourc. Bertrand is his uncle's perpetual lieutenant and is already evoked as being present (though this time as Vivien's companion) at the battle at Orange in which Tedbalt died in Vivien's message in *G1* (ll.672–73) where he is described as a count and 'uns des meillurs de nostre parenté grant'. His role in *ChG* is actually minimal, being replaced, like other notable heroes, by Rainoart, but after being rescued from captivity by him he does play the part of level-headed adviser he so often has next to Guillaume. Needing a horse and armour he asks Rainoart to help him get them, and when the young giant exuberantly swings his club, crushing man and horse, he advises using it like a spear (or billiard cue) to prod the enemy off his horse. The episode is marked by the burlesque humour typical of much of *G2*, with the joke depending on audience recognition of the disjunction between a traditional role and its present application. In *PO* Bertrand suffers the same heroic eclipse as his uncle. Having failed to dissuade him from his scouting mission to Orange, and left in command of the garrison in Nîmes, he laments prematurely over his uncle's death, just as Gillebert arrives to summon his aid, and once before the walls of Orange he despairs of taking the town until Gillebert indicates the existence of a tunnel giving the army access. To him, however, is reserved the honour of despatching the enemy commander, Arragon, although this does little more than underscore the extent to which in the extant *PO* the epic action is a subplot.

Gui is the one character to maintain his epic personality in *PO*, which is perhaps owing to the element of satire or parody evident in his first appearance in *G1*. A *puer-senex* ('old head on young shoulders') he regularly pulls his uncle up short with his 'catch phrase' of 'unques mes n'oi tel' ('I never heard the like'), challenging established wisdom and chivalric convention with a robust common sense that wins the admiration of all. Very much a champion of the younger generation, he sweeps aside the 'leave it to the grown ups' argument with a peremptory 'Ja n'est nul si grant que petit ne fust né' (*ChG*, l.1465). The role he fills, in both *ChG* and *PO*, is very much that of the 'bon larron' who doubles as a magical helper in certain Revolt Cycle and Charlemagne Cycle epics, of whom the most famous is Maugis d'Aigremont, cousin and tireless aid of Renaut de Montauban (*29*). His irrepressible exuberance inspires him to insist on joining Guillaume on the trip to Orange (*AB* ll.382–88) and once there, on each occasion when Guillaume despairs, as when they are trapped in Gloriete, he is ready with his defiance:

> «Niés Guïelin, dist il, quel la ferons?
> Jamés en France, ce cuit, ne revenrons
> Ne ja, neveu, parent ne beserons.[2]
> — Oncle Guillelmes, vos parlez en pardon;
> Que, par l'apostre qu'en quiert en Pré Noiron,
> Ge me cuit vendre ainz que nos descendon.»
> (*AB* 1030–35)

The satirical use of 'common sense' which is his hallmark in *G1* shows in the way he constantly reminds his uncle of the true purpose of his visit, egging him on to make love to Orable now (in prison) that he has ample opportunity and even 'rechristening' him with a fresh nickname: 'Guillelme l'Amïable' (*AB* l.1563). He also shows how (in courtly fashion) a knight should beg his lady to 'secore par amors son amant' (*AB* l.1338), metaphorically going down on his knees and pledging himself to Orable's service, and finishing with the ambiguous plea 'gentill dame, merci!' (*AB*

---

[2]Régnier does not print the first comma in this line, which I have added, since *neveu* is clearly a vocative, not in apposition to *parent*.

l.1356), and yet, when Orable laments that she too has been thrown in prison like a common whore (*AB* l.1552), Gui is again ready with his reply, striking humour from the clash of the literary convention of love as a prison of blissful suffering with the 'reality' of the characters' situation:

> Dist Guïelins: «Vos parlez par folage.
> Vos et mes oncles estes ore en grant ese;
> Par grant amor or devez ce mal trere.»
> (*AB* 1553–55)

The figure who best illustrates the problems of continuity between the different poems is Guibourc. If the reference to her receiving Christianity (*ChG* l.947) is original and not an interpolation added to take account of cyclic developments, it shows that the legend of Guillaume's marriage to a pagan is indeed ancient; Guibourc's own reference to her conversion (l.1422), like the invention of her pagan nephew Guischard, belongs to a later interpolation and is of no account here. However, the reference in the queen's spiteful speech (ll.2591–94) to her being a witch appears to depend on the enchantments conjured up in the early thirteenth-century *Enfances Guillaume*. There is nothing comparable in *PO*, and significantly the passage has no equivalent in *Aliscans*, so is unlikely to have figured in the 'Chanson de Rainoart' from which both it and *G2* probably derive. Elsewhere in *G1* Guibourc acts simply as if she were a noble Christian lady, since she has vassals of her own whom she puts at Guillaume's disposal after the second débâcle at l'Archamp, in fact showing considerable prescience by summoning them in anticipation of disaster (ll.1232–35). She has been responsible for the upbringing of both Gui and Vivien according to *G1*; Vivien sends a particular message to his 'drue' along with those sent to Guillaume (ll.683–88). Moreover she is a tower of strength to the faltering hero at each of the crucial turning points of *ChG* as disaster follows disaster. When Guillaume, anticipating the events of *Le Moniage Guillaume*, announces that it is time for them to retire from the world, she rebels against the suggestion and sends him instead to Paris to raise a new army from the emperor, or at least to get permission to join his household (ll.2410–31). The arrival on the scene of Rainoart modifies Guibourc's role and character considerably, as she is now revealed to be his sister and daughter of the enemy commander Desramé. Her concerns are now mainly for integrating her brother into his new community, providing him with a sword, and at the end of the poem making peace between him and Guillaume, when the latter, acting the part normally given in the cyclic poems to the emperor Louis, has failed to invite to the celebratory feast the man who secured the victory.

In *PO* Guibourc is transformed into the Saracen princess Orable, a name totally unknown to *ChG* which is otherwise so aware of developments in the cyclic poems (but cf. below, p.118). *PO*, like *G2*, remains aloof from the indications of early complicity between Guillaume and Orable found in the *Enfances Guillaume*, and shows the first stirrings of longing in her heart for the hero when Guillaume, disguised as a messenger from her husband, sings the praises of his own martial prowess to her in a setting which endows her with all the erotic exoticism of escapist images of the Orient (*AB* ll.636–736). Although, as we have seen, her stepson, Arragon, paints her as a recalcitrant *mal mariée*, her role in the rest of *PO* is that of the daughter of the emir who in other 'Enamoured Saracen Princess' tales defies her father to rescue from his dungeons the Christian prisoner with whom she has fallen in love, arming him and helping in the conquest of her father's land in the name of the religion she is keen to espouse. Even the incongruously relaxed game of chess that she and Guillaume play at what should be a moment of crisis (*AB* ll.1496–97) belongs to this tradition, as it provides a symbolic representation of prowess in battle (attacking the king) and courtship (attacking the queen). A form of continuity between the poems in the characterisation of Orable-Guibourc is assured, however, by the dynamism of her role in each poem: she provides arms, armour, food, solutions to difficulties and a sense of purpose when the heroes are tempted to drift into despondency.

The similarities and discrepancies we find in the presentation of the different 'characters' in these poems brings back the question of the extent to which we are dealing with the same 'character'. This concerns not only the question of whether the 'Guielin' and 'Guiot', captured in *G1* and *G2* respectively, or the 'Girard' and 'Guischard' who are killed in *G1* are the same or different 'people' from those bearing the same names who figure later in *G2*, but, even more pertinently, whether Guillaume's nephew Guïelin in *PO* can in any way be considered the same 'character' as the 'Guiot' who figures in *ChG* despite the evident similarities of personality presented in each case. Most family trees of the Narbonnais clan established on realist criteria would answer in the negative (*86*). However, realism, as understood by criticism from the mid nineteenth century (*41*), really has no role in the elaboration of epic character, which is a constellation of functions: narrative, symbolic or mythic, socio-cultural (*85*). Which is why in these poems the use to which a character is put — even when that use is a suppression of character or withdrawal of heroic attributes — is more significant than the construction of a self-consistent emotional and psychological persona, and why a 'character' called 'Gui' (with or without diminutive suffixes) or 'Desramé' will for the original audience be the same character when he fulfills the same functions in different poems.

Humour and the Problem of Parody

What I refer to here as 'the problem of parody' might well be considered in the context of medieval studies to be the controversy over parody. Although parody is acknowledged as an autonomous genre in Latin studies (*93*), the very possibility of producing parody in vernacular literature, given the importance of tradition, formula and motif-based composition and the mutability or *mouvance* of 'texts' in both oral and manuscript transmission, has been questioned by a number of critics (*102*, pp.513–21; *83*). A further bar on identifying a medieval work as a parody is raised by Gérard Genette, who adopts a stringent definition requiring the identification of a single specific model before allowing the presence of parody in any piece of writing (*73*, pp.17–25). However, other critics have been happy to apply the notion of parody to individual texts (*106; 90*) or to groups of works (*107*). Moreover the concept of modal or generic parody (*62*, pp.21–22), in which the manipulation of motif and formula challenges the expectations raised by a literary kind and its conventions rather than undercutting a specific work, enables us to conduct an analysis in the terms of the original target audience of the texts.

The application of modern perceptions to medieval formulaic writing and the identification of parody within a surviving work does nevertheless remain a matter of great delicacy and inevitable subjectivity. Robertson's view of *ChG* rests on just such a failure to react to epic stylisation (*128*). Thus his assertion that Vivien's happening to have a silk banner and three gold nails in his leggings to attach it to his lance on Tedbalt's defection (ll.315–19) must be parodic (*114*, pp.21, 26) fails to take account of the formulaic content of this transformation of a simple warrior into a commander. Should one consider Vivien's keeping a banner in his *chalce* as any more comic than Ganelon's using his *hoese* as a safe place to keep the brooches given him by Bramimunde (*17*, ll.634–41), or more improbable than the fact that the lance supplied to Guillaume by Orable is fitted with a pennon held on by five gold nails (*PO, AB* ll.956–57)? A similar question of the perspective provided by modern literary history in judging the intentions of a medieval 'author' affects Lachet's reading of *PO* as 'la parodie courtoise d'une épopée'. Not only does this imply an untenable linear interpretation of twelfth-century literary 'evolution' whereby courtly literature is both more recent than and culturally superior to the epic, but it imposes a monolithic reading of all the constituent elements of the poem. Thus the arms given to Guillaume, including the lance with its silk pennon and gold nails discussed above, are seen as part of the opulent exoticism of the Orient (*90*, pp.70–71), which is both a product of and results in 'une conception plus courtoise et humaniste du monde païen' (*90*, p.78). Not only is the argument circular, but it ignores the luxury and opulence of purely Christian arms: Roland's pennon has gold tassels (*17*, l.1158), Oliver's helmet is studded with gold and gems (*17*, l.1995), Gui l'Allemand has a carbuncle in the nasal of his helmet (*24*, *AB* l.2457), as does his avatar Oton in *Le Charroi de Nîmes* (*20*, l.245), Charlemagne has both a gilded hauberk and a gem-studded helmet (*17*, ll.2499–500). The extent to which all of this is formulaic can be seen from the quintain hung with 'deus haubers safrez' in *Raoul de Cambrai* (*32*, ll.431–32), the fact that in *Le Couronnement de Louis* all characters have a pennon attached to their lance by five gold nails (*24*, *AB* ll.416; 2465; 2078 [fifteen nails]; 2483), and whenever a warrior is hit on the helmet, be he pagan or Christian, the blow dislodges enamelled flowers and precious stones (*24*, *AB* ll.1115–16; 2553–54; 2571–72). All this makes it clear that designating given features of our poems as parodic risks being tendentious. However, it is widely accepted that both contain much burlesque humour, which I shall analyse as such, before considering possible parodic intent, though not necessarily at the expense of the *chanson de geste*.

The question of humour in *ChG* was raised early in critical discussion, since it was considered as a founding monument of French epic poetry, but clearly not of the same austere stamp as the *Roland* (*102*, p.21). This burlesque quality becomes apparent from the very start of the poem in the treatment of Tedbalt. Although his drunkenness may have serious implications (see above, pp.33–35), the presentation of his panic-stricken flight back to Bourges is a model of the grotesque. Critics have concentrated in commenting this episode on Tedbalt's brush with the gallows (ll.338–48) and his ride through a flock of sheep, resulting in his reaching Bourges with just the head of a sheep trapped in his stirrup, the rest of the poor beast having been scattered along the road (ll.395–404: cf. *114*, pp.22–23; *102*, p.40). However, the exchange of words between Tedbalt and his squire, Girard, provides a fine example of the poet's deriving humour from a clash between two versions of the chivalric world. As he flees, and is struck on the face by one of the corpses swinging from the gibbet, Tedbalt dirties himself and his horse's housing, which he proceeds to dump on the road. At the same time he calls back to Girard offering him the cloth:

> Girard apele, quil siwi en la rute:
> 'Ami Girard, car pernez cele hulce;
> Or i ad bon et peres precioses:
> cent livres en purrez prendre a Burges.'
>   (349–52)

At this stage we have no inkling that Girard will be one of the heroes of the song, but his reply, that he can have nothing to do with a sullied housing, gives a hint as to what is to come. More surprising, but equally enigmatic (we never have any way of judging whether Girard is speaking the truth) is his offer to Tedbalt to tell him the whereabouts of a buried treasure he owns, ostensibly so that Tedbalt as overlord can avert a dispute between Girard's heirs (ll.362–64), whereupon the covetous lord of Bourges stops his horse, which the poet castigates as supreme folly. The ironic force of the poet's comment, bizarre in the light of Tedbalt's recent behaviour, is underlined by Girard's throwing him out of the saddle as he had thrown away his soiled housing with the repetition of the verbs *parbute, botat* (ll.348, 368), which also emphasises the source of the humour in the disjunction between the physical and the moral. Tedbalt knows to a penny the price of his cloth, but fails to see that it is a symbol of his own failed career as one of those vainglorious knights more concerned with their parade-ground beauty than with their efficacy as fighters (*31*, II,2; IV,2). By contrast Girard's buried treasure (possibly a symbolic allusion to his as yet unrevealed prowess) gives him access to a real treasure: Tedbalt's arms, and most particularly the shield which was spoils of war, and whose most important feature is not the gold that adorns it, but the glorious history of the clan which it enshrines (ll.374–81).

If there is an underlying seriousness and a harsh satirical edge to the humour marking the Tedbalt-Girard exchanges, the scenes in which Gui appears are notable for pure exuberance. With his constant sharp retorts and a certain vulgar directness ('si aveit coilz', l.1971, he replies to Guillaume's reproach that he has killed a man missing a leg) he represents the unquenchable energy of youth. When his uncle calls on him to show his skill with horse and arms, having set the horse galloping:

> Brandist la hanste desur le braz senestre,
> tote l'enseigne fait venir tresk'en terre;
> il la redresce et le vent la ventele.
> Balçan retient en quatre pez de terre,
> si que la cue li trainad sur l'erbe.
>
> (1664–68)

Yet even in the middle of this dazzling display, the poet stops to remind us that Gui 'Pé et demi ad le cors sur la sele; / a sul trei deie broche desuz la feltre' (ll.1662–63). This diminutive warrior is dwarfed even by the lady's mount lent him by Guibourc, the humour of which is not fully felt until he in turn lends the horse to his uncle, who has had his own horse killed under him.

The interplay of elements at the end of *G1* is very complex. The separation of Guillaume and Gui on the battlefield is presented as an example of the motif of the tragic parting of companions ('Iloec desevrerent entre Willame et Gui', l.1779), normally a signal of death and defeat (cf. *17*, ll.1952–2023; *32*, ll.2463–2555), and which has been invoked in tragic mode in the Vivien section, when Girard leaves to take his message to Guillaume: 'Tendrement plurent andui des oilz de lur vis... Deus, pur quei sevrerent en dolente presse?' (ll.693–95). However, the motivation for this parting is Gui's hunger and thirst (in contrast to Vivien's Christological thirst he needs a snack) and Guillaume sends him to the abandoned Saracen camp with advice to eat plenty and drink little, whereas, ignoring his uncle as usual, 'Mangat del pain — mes ço fut petit; / un grant sester but en haste del vin' (ll.1795–96). The defeat scenario is further developed by the onslaught on the now isolated hero by pagans who kill his horse with javelins, reducing him to the status of foot soldier (ll.1803–07), and then overwhelm him as he tries to fight on, wringing from his lips a desperate call for help (ll.1809–19). This seems closely modelled on Vivien's last stand, though much abbreviated (cf. ll.760–925), until it turns to comedy with the return of Gui (thus further undermining the 'separation of companions' motif), who saves his uncle and the day, driving off the Saracens single-handed — a miracle as the poet observes with a straight face (ll.1858–59). It is at this point that Gui offers his horse to Guillaume, generating first an 'irrelevant' exchange on how Gui acquired the horse — highlighting Gui's impertinence — then a portrait of the mounted warrior which is anti-heroic: Guillaume's inability to control either the horse or his weapons because of the disproportion between the warrior and his mount contrasts sharply with Gui's dexterity in similar conditions:

> Li bers Willame chevalche par le champ,
> sa espee traite, son healme va enclinant.
> Les pez li pendent desuz les estrius a l'enfant;
> a ses garez li vunt les fers batant.
> Et tint sa espee entre le punz et le brant,
> del plat la porte sur sun arçun devant.
> (1880–85)

The same anti-heroic vein runs through what should be the climactic duel with Desramé. The opening of this scene has a feeling of a film running backwards: the pagan commander is found lying in a pool of blood, then leaps to the saddle and spurs his horse to a gallop, charging his foe (ll.1889–99). However, the sight of Guillaume lumbering on his bizarre mount causes him to pull up and approach at a walk (ll.1903–04, repeated with refrain ll.1919–19a). Between the two references to Desramé's approach comes another argument between Guillaume and Gui, who (in a motif also found in *Le Couronnement de Louis* (*24*, *AB* ll.2418–32), where Bertrand takes the role attributed to Gui in *ChG*) claims the duel only to be put down by his uncle. There is in fact no duel. Guillaume is stationary on a woman's horse he cannot control and Desramé merely passing at a walk. As he passes Guillaume strikes him on the helmet with his sword, which should be an epic blow with predictable outcome. On this occasion it simply unbalances the Saracen, who clings to his charger's neck for support, allowing

Guillaume to sever his leg with a sweep of his sword (ll.1920–26). It is impossible to tell whether this account of the climax of the battle of l'Archamp (which presumably replaced a more conventional one in an earlier version of the poem) is based on the duel with Alderufe in *G2* or vice versa. Although the presence of the duel with Aerofle in *Aliscans* would lead us to suspect that the Desramé duel is derivative of that (in its 'Chanson de Rainoart' version), we must remember that the first part of *Aliscans* may itself be based on material now lost from the original *ChG*, so that a closed circle of reciprocal influence is not impossible. Perhaps both recall in burlesque mode the duel with the giant Corsolt in *Le Couronnement de Louis*, who is so big and powerful that a first blow delivered by Guillaume with Joyeuse merely stuns him: the hero has to use both hands on the sword to deliver the blow which decapitates him (*AB* ll.1090–1136). In any case we note that the humour associated with Guillaume is of a dark and sarcastic kind (not unlike that directed earlier at Tedbalt and Esturmi), while the humour associated with Gui remains light and invigorating.

There is a similarly positive air to the humour surrounding Rainoart in *G2* despite the violence associated with much of it (*102*, pp.69–73). We may consider such humour archaic and brutal, but it is the essence of such cartoon characters as Bugs Bunny or Popeye the Sailor, and serves as a means of sublimating urges which would otherwise produce unbearable tensions in the individual and society. To a great extent Rainoart, like his twentieth-century cartoon counterparts, and the laughter they generate, belongs to the carnival or *charivari* which is both a safety-valve and a means of renewal (*43*, pp.12–16).

Unlike in *Aliscans*, where his arrival and signal part in the Christian victory is announced long before we see him, Rainoart's entry in *G2* is unprepared, and the audience may be expected to take him at face value. His connection with the kitchen and 'low life' is therefore a given of his character until the final revelation of his royal origins at the end of the poem. When not explicitly associated with the kitchen (where he prefers to sleep, shunning a bed prepared by Guibourc, ll.2859–67) he is presented as a fool (in the technical sense of a 'jester') by the 'club' he carries over his shoulder and his 'black' and tattered appearance. It is therefore natural that the humour associated with him relates repetitively to these functions, and gets its effect by reiteration, provoking a sense of the mechanical (*56*, pp.30–37). In addition to his killing of the head cook who insulted him (ll.2670–91) he is twice made drunk by kitchen-boys and wreaks deadly vengeance on them (ll.2695–717; 2867–95). However, the mechanical aspect of the repetition is softened by variations in each passage. In the first the scullions hide his *tinel* in a haystack, and on recovering it after killing two of his tormentors Rainoart brandishes it, as a chivalric hero would his lance, and threatens the pagan enemy: 'N'en guarrad pé, quant jo ai le tinel' (l.2717). In the second he goes quietly to sleep (using the corpse of one of his victims as a pillow and cuddling up to his *tinel* as if it were some soft toy, ll.2893–95). The next morning he summons the sluggard Frankish knights to battle shouting the imperial war cry:

> 'Munjoie!' escrie, 'Frans chevalers, muntez!'
> (2898)

which can be compared to Girard's departure (ll.1070–74) or Guillaume's (ll.1495–97). When this produces only grumbling (the Franks complain that the cock has crowed only twice, eliciting the retort from Rainoart that he has given it his orders, ll.2904–05[3]) he drives them out in terror, threatening to demolish Guillaume's great hall about their ears with his *tinel* (ll.2910–13). Further complaints about this addressed to Guillaume, general cursing of the over-eager recruit, and calls for him to be given a good thrashing, bring the explanation that he is a licensed fool, and it is not their place to threaten him (ll.2925–26). The comedy is that of the clown, who

---

[3] Or possibly 'ordered you to do it', i.e. 'get up'. The pronoun already liable to ambiguity in Continental French of the twelfth century becomes much more uncertain for a thirteenth-century insular audience. It is notable that this episode is peculiar to *G2* and does not figure in *Al*, so may be of insular origin.

wreaks havoc with the lives of more sober citizens, and whose 'purloining' of language or gesture 'belonging' to those 'better classes' we see as parodic or burlesque because of his pre-assigned role in literature or society.

The same mixture of repetition and burlesque is found in another of Rainoart's exploits. After he has rescued the prisoners from the Saracen boats, Bertrand asks him to find them arms. That he wishes to take them from fallen enemies is not strange in the context of medieval warfare; that he decides to kill fresh enemies rather than despoil those already dead is unusual. This does, of course, permit the humour of his delivering repeated epic blows with his *tinel*, which render the arms useless, since instead of slicing man and horse in two (as is described in the 'classic' epic blow with a sword) he squashes rider, mount and equipment to a pulp (ll.3081–99), leading Bertrand to expostulate 'Se si vus vient, jo n'erc huimés adubé. / Issi en poez quatre mil tuer!' (ll.3100–01) and to ask deferentially if Rainoart couldn't kill them by prodding them. Rainoart's reply of 'I never thought of that' (l.3113) reminds us that we are dealing with the traditional double act of clown and straight man. This effect is further exaggerated in *Aliscans*, where Rainoart first tells the Franks to take arms from fallen Saracens and is then asked to get them horses by Bertrand, who has to remind Rainoart twice about his advice to 'prod' before the lesson is learnt (7, ll.5616–807).

The same element of repetition is found at the heart of much of the humour in *PO*. Apart from the systematic exploitation of formulaic composition, giving the poem its indelibly epic stamp (see above, pp.71–73), the narrative is shot through with recurring motifs. One such is the *prière du plus grand péril*, which springs to Guillaume's lips at the slightest provocation. The first comes when, safely disguised and under no suspicion, he hears Arragon boast of what he would do to Guillaume if he captured him (*AB* ll.491–509). This is followed by similar appeals for divine protection at ll.540–44 (a repetition of the previous scene), ll.781–90 and 804–17 (when Salatré wipes off his make-up and Arragon threatens to execute him). Restricted to the first half of the poem, the sense of intense repetition is generated by grouping them in 'parallel' pairs, and associating them with the equally recurrent motif of Arragon's blustering threats. This is additionally stressed by the formulaic rigidity of the last couplet of each:

> 'Gardez noz cors de mort et de torment,
> Ne nos ocïent Sarrazin et Persant.'
> > (*AB* 508–09)

> 'Garis mon cors de mort et de prison,
> Ne nos ocïent cist Sarrazin felon.'
> > (*AB* 515–16)

> 'Garis mon cors de mort et d'afoler,
> Ne nos ocïent Sarrazin et Escler.'
> > (*AB* 789–90)

> 'Deffendez nos de mort et de prison,
> Ne nos ocïent cist Sarrazin felon.'
> > (*AB* 816–17)

The argument that the prayers are a mark of the hero's simple piety is undermined by their being preceded by signs of unwonted poltroonery on Guillaume's part, expressed in equally mechanical terms:

> Guillelmes l'ot, si se vet enbronchant,
> Mielz volsist estre a Paris ou a Sanz...
> > (*AB* 496–97)

> Guillelmes l'ot, si tint le chief enbron,
> Lors vosist estre a Rains ou a Loon...
> > (*AB* 538–39)

> Voit le Guillelmes, le sens cuide desver,
> Trestot le sanc del cors li est müé...
> > (*AB* 780–81)

Guillelmes l'ot, si taint comme charbon;
Dont vosist estre a Rains ou a Loon…
(*AB* 800–01)

Moreover, if the prayers disappear from the second half of the poem, the references to Guillaume's 'loss of moral fibre' do not (cf. *AB* 904–08; 1030–32; 1055–56; 1186–87; 1193–94 etc.). Though they are interspersed with rare moments of defiance from the hero (*AB* ll.607–11; 876–78; 880–86), they mostly act to provide a foil for Gui's belligerent sarcasm, underscoring the fact that, as with Rainoart and Bertrand in *G2-Aliscans*, we are again dealing with a classic double act.

This particular feature seems not to have been inherited from the cyclic archetype, but to be an invention of the *AB* redactor. Of the four prayers mentioned above only one, the last, is found presented in full in the *C* and *D* redactions, where in both cases it is attributed to Gui, not to Guillaume. The second and third are totally omitted in the other redactions, and *C* actually increases the heroic atmosphere by having Gui wish for weapons to teach the Saracens a lesson (*C* ll.574–77). Likewise the first of the prayers, the most incongruous in *AB*, is omitted by *D*, although *C* keeps a couplet in indirect speech giving a résumé of the prayer ('Reclama Dieu, le pere omnipotent, / K'il le defende de paine et de torment', ll.478–79) which suggests that the mechanical repetitions tending to comedy were present in their common ancestor, being exaggerated by *AB* and reduced by *C*.

Taken alone this abuse of the *prière du plus grand péril* might not be seen as funny, or even significant: it could be argued that even an epic hero might be given the benefit of the doubt in a difficult situation, provided that he does not, like Tedbalt and Estourmi, cave in completely. It is, however, as part of a complex of such abused motifs that it operates to suggest a subversive interpretation for the poem. One such is that of the escape from captivity. Gillebert escapes from Orange (*AB* ll.117–26 and 217–26) with astounding ease, having been released from his chains by a gaoler before a beating is to be administered; Guillaume, in his persona of a Saracen messenger sent by Tiebaut, pretends to have escaped from Nîmes (*AB* ll.481–90) or to have been let go by Guillaume, who is so powerful he is indifferent to prisoners, while Salatré really has escaped from Nîmes (*AB* ll.748–51), although the narrator admits his ignorance as to how this was accomplished. Then, of course, there are the two 'escapes' from prison of Guillaume and his companions in Orange (*AB* ll.1384–86 and 1587–88), which again are not really escapes, since in the first instance Orable walks out with the Franks unopposed, and in the second the Saracens haul Guillaume and Gui out of their dungeon (leaving Orable behind) when they hear them squabbling. This last example reminds us that these escapes are merely conveniences of the narrator, and might lead us to apply to *PO* Frappier's description of *Le Charroi de Nîmes* as 'un roman de cape et d'épée' (*72*, 2, p.195). However, the mechanical regularity of their use generates at least a sense of euphoria in the narration, and most probably a feeling of hilarity.

This feeling is reinforced by the employment of secret tunnels not only for escape (even Salatré uses a 'fosse' to leave Nîmes) but also for capture. Every time the heroes think they are safe, every time the Saracens think they have the Franks under lock and key, another tunnel opens up to give the other side access or egress. They are also a means for the narrator to demonstrate his artistic manipulation of the plot, and so undermine any seriousness that might remain in the poem, as the escape engineered by Orable from the first dungeon, when Gillebert is sent away to fetch reinforcements demonstrates. This leads to the most illogical (but 'necessary') return of Guillaume, Gui and Orable to Glorïete, where all three idle away their time playing the ultimate courtly game of chess (*AB* ll.1467–99). By no clearer means could the narrator signal the ludic dimension of his creation.

Although most of the poet's humour seems to be aimed at epic motifs, and to those considered above we can add the arming-knighting of the hero, the fight with unconventional arms, the *planctus*, much sport is also derived from the fitting into a strict epic mould of such courtly motifs as the *raverdie*, love sickness provoked by *amor de lonh*, love as a prison and the petition to the Lady. This poem is the product of a very sophisticated author who had full command of all the types of literature currently popular in his society. He clearly sets his sights much higher than merely parodying an epic, or even the epic; indeed it is hard to see *PO* as parody except in a very diluted sense (*118*, p.600), and it is probably more profitable to see it as a playful compilation (cf. *66*, pp.455–57; *44*) of the sort that *Aucassin et Nicolette* will be a generation or so later. The humour, parodic only in the original sense of requiring a literary point of comparison to be appreciated, does not appear to be critical or designed to undermine any particular cultural perceptions.

The same is not true of *ChG*, although the criticism is not necessarily aimed at literary models as Robertson believes (*114*). The complex history of the production of *ChG* as we find it in the extant manuscript also means that different parts of the poem take varying approaches. While the first 900 lines seem to satirise secular chivalry in the name of the rising ideology of the *militia Christi* of the Templars and Hospitalers, the next 1,000 lines do appear to target conventional literary heroism, particularly in the person of Guillaume d'Orange. The last part of the poem (*G2*) takes a different tack again, presenting a burlesque of the epic in the name of a cultural renewal through the conjunction of Guibourc and Rainoart. The heroic and moral lack posited at the beginning of *G2*, and found also in the revised parts of *G1* (cf. *112*, pp.35–38), is satisfied, and that making-whole celebrated, in the baptism of Rainoart, as the more explicitly expressed lacks of Guillaume's life (harpers, *jongleurs*, women to disport with and Saracens to fight, *AB* ll.54–69) are fully satisfied and celebrated at the wedding feast of the hero and Orable, baptised as Guibourc (*AB* ll.1862–85). However the last lines of *PO* remind us that a life of tribulation and the bloody events of l'Archamp-Aliscans lie ahead for the hero and his gaily won spouse:

> Li cuens Guillelmes ot espousé la dame;
> Puis estut il tiex .xxx. anz en Orenge

C'onques un jor n'i estut sanz chalenge.
(*AB* 1886–88)

The Capture of Orange: The Evolution of a Theme

Despite the historic victories of Guillaume, Count of Toulouse, Charlemagne's cousin and military 'tutor' to the young Louis, King of Aquitaine, in south-west France and Catalonia (culminating in 803 in the capture of Barcelona and the establishment of the Spanish March), and despite the poetic beauties of *ChG*, it was the entirely fictitious capture of Orange which came to dominate his legend. If his original nickname of 'Guillaume al curb nés' was replaced by that of 'Guillaume au court nez' in the cyclic texts following the injury received in battle with Corsolt in *Le Couronnement de Louis* (*24*, *AB*, ll.1030–44), he is more generally known, in poems from *Aliscans* onwards, and universally to modern critics, as 'Guillaume d'Orange' from the name of the town which replaced Barcelona as his capital in the cyclic texts.

The reasons for the transfer of the focus of the legend from the trans-Pyrenean region to the Rhône Valley remain obscure. The pull of the Roman remains of Avignon, Arles and Nîmes, as well as those of Orange itself, have been given credit for this (*74*; *72*, 2, pp.272–78; *63*), but the cases made out are not totally convincing. On the one hand it is arbitrary to assume that more westerly remains, such as those at Narbonne (a town associated with the epic of Guillaume's father Aymeri), were less evocative than those further east; on the other hand from the mid-eleventh century, and increasingly in the twelfth, Roman remains had to compete in the imagination of the audience for *chansons de geste* with the splendours of Muslim civilisation seen in Spain and in the Middle East. When one considers that the magnetic power of the name *Espagne* was such that in the Old French epic it refers to the vast area spreading from Spain proper across southern France into northern Italy, the easterly transfer seems highly illogical. There is, however, one late Roman monument that seems to have contributed significantly to the process, having itself an awesome appeal to the imagination which is not altogether dissipated today.

The great cemetery of the Aliscans at Arles was a Christian burying place in use from the fourth century. It contains relics of a number of martyrs and confessors of southern Gaul, and had within its boundaries several sanctuaries recommended to the attention of pilgrims. Towards the middle of the twelfth century there grew up the legend that this was the site of an apocalyptic battle involving Christian Frankish heroes. The slain were considered martyrs and were buried on the site of their martyrdom. This legend is the foundation of *Aliscans*, surviving in a version dating from the 1190s, but, as we have seen, deriving from a poem that must have been extant in the 1150s. However, this view of the early-Christian cemetery was far from universal in the mid-twelfth century, and there is simply no mention of it as a resting place for 'epic' heroes in the *Liber Sancti Jacobi*, a guide book to the pilgrim route to Compostela composed probably in the 1140s. For this writer the Aliscans is merely a sacred site at which the pilgrim should be sure to pray, and, despite his willingness to exploit the epic associations of Roncevaux, he evokes no such heroic memories here. More significantly the *Vita Sancti Willelmi*, the earliest text to mention Guillaume's capture of Orange, likewise makes no reference to the cemetery. The first text to show clearly the influence of the legend is the *Historia Karoli Magni et Rotolandi* (commonly known today as the *Pseudo-Turpin Chronicle*, since the anonymous author adopts the persona of the Archbishop of Reims from the *Roland*, cf. *15*, pp.86–87), although this 'chronicle' causes heroes killed at Roncevaux to be transported to Arles for burial and knows nothing of heroes slain on the site itself.

In the light of this it seems unlikely that place alone was responsible for the removal of Guillaume from Languedoc to Provence. We need, therefore, to consider additionally whether contamination with other historical characters might not have been responsible. Such a conclusion was the natural corollary of nineteenth-century Traditionalist criticism, which derived *chansons de geste* from short, ballad-like songs, each of which may have had a different hero. It was against such theories, which he had espoused earlier in his career, that Joseph Bédier (*47*, 1, pp.180–205) reacted, pouring the full weight of his rhetorical scorn on the 'seize Guillaumes' his predecessors saw contributing to the character of Guillaume d'Orange. Now, while Bédier was undoubtedly right to criticise the idea that every incident in Guillaume's legend had to have a historical precedent, and hence an identifiable prototype, he was unfair in simply adding up all the alternative suggestions that had been made for some episodes to reach his inflated total. Current criticism, moreover, has returned to the notion that both contamination and duplication are common features of the generation of an epic biography in many literatures (*124*, pp.138–40). In that light one cannot discount the suggestion that both William, Count of Avignon, who defended the Rhône Valley against Muslim and Viking pirates in the tenth century, and St Vidian or Vezian from south-west France, conflated with the Vivien, Count of Tours, who died in battle against the Bretons in 853, may have helped the legend of Guillaume 'al curb nez' to crystallise around the cemetery of Aliscans (*72*, 1, pp.66 n.1, 183 n.2; *131*, 1, pp.509–30). However, what remains a mystery, for all the ingenuity applied to the problem has not produced a satisfactory account, is why Guillaume became not Guillaume d'Arles (or des Aliscans) but precisely Guillaume d'Orange (cf. however *72*, 2, pp.274–78, which applies to Orange and its Roman antiquities arguments also applied to other sites).

Whatever theories may be advanced in explanation, it remains a fact that by ca 1122, long before the proto-*Aliscans* was produced, Guillaume was associated with capturing Orange from the Muslims. This is found in the *Vita* of St William of Gellone, where we read:

> Itaque Willelmus Dux salutatus a Carolo, et ipse pio Domino benignum vale faciens, procedit, fortem et electum producit exercitum; itaque Septimaniam ingressus, transito quoque Rhodano, ad urbem concitus Arausicam agmina et castra (quam illi Hispani cum suo Theobaldo jampridem occupavererunt) ipsam facile ac brevi caesis atque fugatis eripit invasoribus, licet postea

et in ea et pro ea multos et longos ab hostibus labores
pertulerit, semperque praevaluerit decertando.

(*38*, Maii, 6, p.800D-E)[4]

This factually dry account taken from the Church's official
biography of the saint is shot through with signs of epic influence.
Firstly, the expedition, which proceeds from the unidentified site of
the imperial court, is literally blessed by Charles, which, while re-
establishing proper historical chronology for William by removing
him from the reign of Charles's son Louis, has the emperor acting
as he does in the *Roland*, for instance, when he sends Ganelon on
his ill-fated mission (*17*, ll.339–40). Then the invaders, who are
quickly dislodged from Orange, are said to be 'Spaniards' (we
should understand 'Moors') commanded by a man with an unlikely
Germanic name: Theobaldus. Although it was not unknown for
Moors to employ non-Muslim commanders (the most famous being
Rodrigo de Bibar, el Cid), it is more likely that we are here dealing
with the phenomenon well known to Old French epic of conflating
all the enemies of western Europe under the general heading of
'pagans' and that the presence of the man referred to by Vivien as
'Tedbalt l'Esturman' (*ChG*, l.667) and who emerges in later epics
as Tiebaut, Orable's first husband, represents a memory of the
activities of Frisian or Viking pirates.

The clearest link between the hagiographic text and surviving
epics is the reference to the trials or labours that William had to
endure in defence of his conquest. This appears to be the first
allusion to what has survived in a highly romanticised form in
manuscript *E* of *PO* as the 'Siège d'Orange', and in redactions *AB*
(ll.1887–88) and *C* (ll.2285–88) as the thirty (or sixty) years of

---

[4] 'Thus Duke William, with Charles's blessing, and himself bidding a fond
farewell to his pious lord, went forth leading a strong, élite army; and thus
entering Septimania and crossing the Rhône with a mighty thrust, he
pitched camp at the town of Orange (which at that time the Spanish held
with their leader Theobald), and he snatched the same quickly and easily
from the invaders who were either killed or fled. Afterwards, within the
town and in order to defend it, he had to endure many long trials at the
hands of the enemy, and always prevailed in the fight.'

conflict which Guillaume endured daily to preserve his conquest. *C* notably uses the word 'paines' (l.2287), a good rendering of the Latin 'labores', saying that they ended only with Guillaume's definitive victory at Aliscans (where by implication the defeated pagan commander is again Tiebaut not Desramé). The siege of Orange is also incorporated in *Aliscans* (*laisses* 49–50, 55–56 and 80), where the besieging army is jointly commanded by Tiebaut and Desramé, although the former disappears from the scene again before battle is joined at Aliscans. What is missing from the Latin text, in terms of the established patterns of the Guillaume Cycle, is any reference either to Orable-Guibourc or to any member of the Narbonnais clan in the hero's army.

This latter absence is repaired in the earliest reference we have to the events in a surviving poem. When Vivien is sending Girard for help from his uncle in *ChG* (ll.628 ff.) and reminding him of the debts of gratitude he has to his nephew, particular mention is made of the 'great battle beneath the walls of Orenge' in which Tedbalt 'the Steersman' (i.e. the shipmaster or navigator) was killed (ll.666–75). While this passage, like the rest of the 'biography' of Vivien used to construct the appeal to Guillaume, must be an innovation in *ChG* reassigning to the young hero exploits attributed to other heroes of the *geste* in other songs (*72*, 2, pp.270–71), it does mesh firmly with the data about the fall of Orange contained in cyclical poems post-1150. There are obvious differences between the extant *PO* and Vivien's account (Gui is not present in the latter, while Bernard de Brubant is, and Tiebaut, far from being absent, is present and actually killed), but the presence at Guillaume's side of his constant lieutenant Bertrand, who fills this role in *Le Couronnement de Louis* and *Le Charroi de Nîmes* as well as in *PO*, shows that the allusion is firmly rooted in that very cyclic tradition.

Nor is it necessary to posit, as Frappier suggests (not without whimsicality, *72*, 2, p.271) that the reference in the *Vita* is not to the capture but to the subsequent siege of the city. The killing of the ruler of the conquered city is a commonplace of the epic, exemplified in the death of Borel in the eleventh-century 'Hague Fragment', which is generally seen as the transposition of an early poem related to the Guillaume cycle (*72*, 1, pp.69–76). Although neither the city being attacked nor the hero is identified in the 'Fragment', the exploit bears some resemblance to one assigned to Vivien in *ChG* where not Borel himself but his twelve sons are killed in a battle at Gerona (ll.374–76) or Saragossa (ll.635–42). Similarly Harpin and Otrant, joint kings of Nîmes, are killed in *Le Charroi de Nîmes* (*20*, ll.1374–79 and 1456–63). So the reference in the *Vita* and its reworking in *ChG* could be to a very early state of *PO*. However, given that the episode shows the general tendency of the reviser of *G1* to demote Guillaume in favour of a series of younger heroes, it is fair to conclude that the allusion belongs to that state of the text current ca 1150. In that case it is highly likely that the reviser knew a version of the *PO* in which Guillaume not only conquered the city, but, like many other heroes of epic and romance, a bride.

The identification of this bride with Orable-Guibourc seems likewise to date from the mid-century at the earliest. It is only in an episode unique to *ChG* (ll.2823–25 and 2873–74, cf. *131*, 1, p.713), in which Rainoart reveals his own parentage, that we learn that his mother (and by implication Guibourc's mother) was called Oriabel, a name parallel to Orable and similarly referring to Orange, presupposing the existence of that name in the tradition by the time *G2* was being formulated as a continuation of and new conclusion to *G1*. Certainly the name appears in *Le Charroi de Nîmes*, a text probably dating from the late 1150s or 1160s, in connection with Orable's marriage to Tiebaut (*20*, ll.521–22). Since it is widely accepted that *Le Charroi de Nîmes* was written solely to provide a prelude to the *PO*, it may be that it was in this period of the constitution of the kernel of the cycle (*82*, pp.35–37) that it was felt necessary to bring together the disparate parts of Guillaume's legend by identifying the heroine of the capture of Orange with the heroic spouse who contributes so much to the Vivien-Aliscans part of the cycle.

The extant *PO* comprises two essential motifs. The first is the visit of the disguised hero to the enemy's camp; the second that of the Saracen princess in love with the Christian hero (*126*; *52*). The former has two manifestations, since the hero's penetration of the enemy stronghold can be either for reconnaissance (as in *Gui de Bourgogne*, where Charlemagne disguised as a pilgrim reconnoitres the rebels' camp in person, cf. *98*, pp.129, 137, 340) or to facilitate conquest (as in *Le Charroi de Nîmes*, where Guillaume and his army dress as merchants to take the pagan garrison by surprise, cf. *20*, ll.1036ff.). In *PO* we find a mixture of these motifs, probably caused by the grafting of a new poem, in which the avowed object of the journey is to see how beautiful Orable really is, on to an older stock concerned purely with conquest. There can be no question of Guillaume's conquering Orange with just two companions, even in this frequently comic text, where the trio do succeed in clearing Glorïete of an army of Saracen defenders. In fact the poet of the extant text keeps the two versions of the motif in parallel, to the extent that it is ultimately Bertrand who conquers Orange (and kills Tiebaut's surrogate, Arragon), Guillaume contenting himself with freeing Orable from her prison (ll.1796–1851). Thus far the current version accords with Vivien's message in *G1*, further reinforced in the *C* redaction by the fact that the bulk of the final battle is fought not within the town, after Bertrand has been led through the underground passage by Gillebert, but 'Devant les portes d'Orenge la chité' (*C* 1.2131).

The second motif, that of the Enamoured Princess, is itself a late romantic development of an older folk motif of mythological origin whereby the sovereignty of the place to be conquered passes with possession of the female principle, which may explain why Orable is never supplied with a clearly defined father figure (*100*; *131*, 1, pp.543–47, 711–15). As manifested in most epics of the late twelfth and early thirteenth centuries, it represents a mixture of exoticism and naïve sexual wish-fulfilment, sanctioned by the young lady's willingness to convert to Christianity and betray family and people to a higher cause. Unlike the heroines of other epics, who see the hero in battle or learn about him from a third party, Orable seems to learn first of Guillaume's existence from his own lips after he has entered Glorïete in disguise and boasts of his wealth, power and prowess to her (ll.694–717 and 725–30). The sigh that this

draws from her (l.718), like the thought that the lady he loved
would be happy (l.733) and the tears of pity she weeps (l.941), may
all be steps in the growth of love, but her attitude remains highly
equivocal, threatening the Christians and inviting them to surrender
until she finally strikes her clear bargain with Guillaume:

> — En moie foi, dist la roïne Orable,
> Se ge cuidoie que ma paine fust sauve,
> Que me preïst Guillelmes Fierebrace,
> Ge vos metroie toz trois hors de la chartre,
> Si me feroie crestïenner a haste.»
>
> (*AB* 1374–78)

Despite even this avowal Guillaume and, more especially, Guïelin,
remain sceptical about Orable's intentions to the end. Equally
significant in this context may be the fact that whereas in most
poems presenting an Enamoured Princess she is the unmarried
daughter of the pagan commander (possibly betrothed to an older
Saracen warrior to whom she prefers the young Christian), Orable is
the wife of the enemy ruler.

It is these discrepancies between the Enamoured Princess
motif as it is regularly exploited in later *chansons de geste* and the
use made of it in *PO* which invite further reflection on the poet's
parallel exploitation of the earlier manifestation of the story-type.
We know from other sources that originally the capture of Orange
was a bloody affair fought out directly between Guillaume and
Tiebaut. Furthermore, allusions in *Foucon de Candie*, *Aliscans* and
the *Moniage Guillaume* reveal a dark and brutal side to both
Guillaume and Orable in the massacre of the children of Orable's
marriage to Tiebaut. In the late *Foucon de Candie* it is Tiebaut
himself, who, having survived the conquest in keeping with the
cyclic tradition, reproaches his former wife for her part in the events
(cf. *72*, 1, pp.262–63):

> «Ahi! Orable! ce dist li Arrabiz,
> Mauvaise feme renoiee et meltriz,

> Par vos fui ge premierement traïz.
> Vos me tollistes Orenge as murs voutiz.
> Enz accollistes Guillelme et ses norriz.
> Malement m'a de mes filz departiz:
> Prist en les testes sor un perron voutiz.
> Feme est deables et ses faiz et ses diz.»
>
> (9474–82)

This passage shows the poet of *Foucon de Candie* in some difficulties reconciling the Medea-like role of an Orable killer of her own children with a tradition that it was Guillaume who slew them. This view of events prevails in *Aliscans* where Guillaume justifies his actions to another surviving son, Esmeré, who addresses him as 'paratre' (l.1242):

> Respont Guillelmes: «Vos dites cruauté!
> Puisque li hom n'aime crestïenté
> Et qu'il het Deu et despit carité
> n'a droit en vie, jel di par verité;
> Et qui l'ocist, si destruit un maufé;
> Deu a vengié, si l'en set mout bon gré.
> Tuit estes chien par droiture apelé,
> car vos n'avez ne foi ne lëauté.»
>
> (7, 1255–62)

Now this highly aggressive stance which belongs strictly to the military, crusading literature of the twelfth and thirteenth centuries (*116*, pp.52–57, 94–99, 215–23) becomes unconvincing in the light of the conversions of Rainoart and Orable, not to mention her nephew Guischard in *G1*. Nevertheless the grimness of the fate of all males connected with Orange before Guillaume's arrival seems incontestable in the early tradition, and since it is so meticulously softened in the existing version of *PO* where Tiebaut is removed from the conflict to be replaced by a grotesque bugbear, and Orable is presented as a childless courtly lady, we need to look beyond the surviving text to elucidate the model on which it is built.

This is to be found in the archetypal tale of the conquest by the hero of sovereignty (personified by a female) and the killing of the previous ruler. The story type, transmitted from Celtic sources, is highly prevalent in Arthurian romance. A particularly clear example is furnished by Chrétien's *Yvain*, in which the hero conquers Laudine and becomes master of her realm having first killed her previous husband and then gained access to her tower through the agency of a magic ring given him by Laudine's maid-in-waiting, Lunete. To complete the pattern, it is made clear (*27*, ll.2103–06) that the 'custom' of Laudine's marrying the victor in successive battles has been established for 'more than sixty years', which, taken in conjunction with the seven years separating Calogrenant's defeat from Yvain's victory, suggests a 'magical' figure meaning 'time out of mind'. The pattern can be compared with that found in the early annals of Ireland, in which, over a period of about 200 years each king succeeds following the violent death of his predecessor, each new king taking as wife the queen, Medb, 'Reward': cf. English 'Mead' (*11*, p.7; cf. 52, p.6 n.17).

The reviser who introduced 'Orable' into the story of the capture of Orange could have taken the figure from a tale recounted by one of the many Celtic storytellers active in France from the early twelfth century, but such a source is not essential, since the myth is extremely widespread. Another version of it that the poet of *PO* could have known is that contained in the story of Jason and Medea. Like Orable Medea is of 'barbarian' stock, a witch versed in magic potions and holder of the key to a life-token: the Golden Fleece. She herself is also a giver of life and power and passes from king to king, killing two of her own children by Jason at one point. Her story would have been known in the twelfth century not only in the Latin of Ovid but, from the mid-1150s in Benoît de Sainte-Maure's version in the *Roman de Troie* (*8*, ll.1211–2078).

A further complication in the highly composite cyclic version of *PO* is that the conquest of sovereignty is again crossed with the equally well-known epic motif of the conquest of the Kingdom of the Dead to rescue a frequently feminine life-principle to secure the future of the hero's group (*51*; *52*). Depending on the culture adopting this tale-type the exploit may be accomplished by physical force or by intellectual cunning. In either case disguise may be a prerequisite of eluding the guardians of this 'supernatural' realm, although in this version all the most threatening aspects of the pagan Other World (its entrances and exits, its terrifying rulers and guardians) are reduced to the level of props for a melodrama. Again both variants are exploited in combination here. Firstly the Christian heroes enter and leave Orange by underground passage or water and trick their way past its guardian (all motifs associated with access to the Underworld). They then enter Glorïete, clearly Orable's personal domain, which takes on a particularly paradisal form with its magical tree — a symbol of life (ll.652–56), where the queen is hieratically fanned by a young attendant using a 'platel d'argent' (l.665). While this might suggest an opulent exoticism, such fans were reserved for liturgical use in twelfth-century Europe and for most hearers would evoke a religious atmosphere. This reading of *AB* with its heavy insistence on religion and paradise is confirmed by *D* (ll.521–44 and 553–63), and *a contrario* by the deviant *C* (ll.626–34), which suppresses the reference to fanning and replaces Guillaume's repeated assertion 'paradis est ceanz / ceanz est paradis' (*AB* ll.676 and 688) with the blandly orthodox 'Or m'est issi samblant / Com se j'estoie lasus el fiermament' (*C* ll.659–60). In *C* the secular, courtly scene is set in an exotic enclosed garden with its central gazebo (cf. above, pp.81–82) which Crusaders and other travellers would have seen in Muslim Spain and the Middle East. Whatever the setting (otherworldly paradise or exotic garden, cf. *88*, pp.304–06), Orable is now established as the true authority figure, and trickery is replaced by martial action. However, for the final conquest of the lady the poet reverts to the motif of the assault on the Underworld, with the Frankish army penetrating the fortress through a tunnel, but resolves the issue through a battle of surrogates — Bertrand representing his uncle and Arragon his father.

The evolution of the theme of the capture of Orange is thus subject to constant romanticisation and edulcoration. Starting as a bloody battle to repulse invaders it soon became entangled in the prevailing twelfth-century epic themes of the extension of the Imperium (both Capetian and papal) through crusades and of the renewal of the kingdom. With the further shift in ethos caused by the popularisation of Classical and Celtic themes from the 1150s the figure of Orable seems to have been introduced. Owing to the archetypal origins of this figure, however, the song appears to have remained dark and brutal. Only in the cyclic version of the 1190s, influenced by the lyricism of *fin'amor* and the lighter tones of courtly romance post-Chrétien de Troyes, and shot through with a playful spirit of parody which allows the illogicalities of the song brazen prominence, at least in the *AB* redaction, do we find the complex and sophisticated literary artefact we know today. Like the later parts of *ChG*, but unlike the story of Vivien's gory martyrdom, the surviving *PO* has severed its links with the celebratory aspects of its epic past, no doubt sacrificing some grandeur on the way, and become entertainment for a refined, leisured class prepared to look askance at its own traditions.

Bibliography

This bibliography lists only items referred to in the body of the study. For comprehensive coverage consult Robert Bossuat, *Manuel bibliographique de la littérature française du moyen âge* (Paris, 1951 and supplements) and the *Bulletin Bibliographique de la Société Rencesvals*, published annually since 1958.

EDITIONS AND TRANSLATIONS OF LA CHANSON DE GUILLAUME AND LA PRISE D'ORANGE

1. *La Chançun de Guillelme*, ed. Hermann Suchier, Bibliotheca Normannica, 8 (Halle, Niemeyer, 1911).
2. *La Chanson de Guillaume*, ed. Duncan McMillan, 2 Vols, Société des Anciens Textes Français (Paris, Picard, 1949–50).
3. *La Chanson de Guillaume*, ed. & trans. François Suard, Classiques Garnier (Paris, Bordas, 1991; nouvelle édition, 1999).
4. *La Chanson de Guillaume*, ed. & trans. Philip E. Bennett (London, Grant & Cutler, 2000).
5. *Les Rédactions en vers de la Prise d'Orange*, ed. Claude Régnier (Paris, Klincksieck, 1966).
6. *La Prise d'Orange éditée d'après la rédaction AB*, ed. Claude Régnier, Bibliothèque Française et Romane, B5 (Paris, Klincksieck, 2nd ed.1969).

EDITIONS AND TRANSLATIONS OF OTHER MEDIEVAL TEXTS

7. *Aliscans*, ed. Claude Régnier, 2 Vols, Classiques Français du Moyen Age, 110–111 (Paris, Champion, 1990).
8. Benoist de Sainte-Maure, *Le Roman de Troie*, ed. Léopold Constans, 6 Vols, Société des Anciens Textes Français (Paris, Didot, 1904–12).
9. *Beowulf*, trans. Michael Alexander, The Penguin Classics (Harmondsworth, Penguin Books, 1973).
10. Beroul, *The Romance of Tristran*, ed. A. Ewert, 2 Vols (Oxford, Blackwell, 1939 & 1970).

11.   *Early Irish Myths and Sagas*, trans. Jeffrey Gantz, Penguin Classics (Harmondsworth, Penguin Books, 1981).

12.   *Fierabras*, ed. A. Kroeber and G. Servois, Les Anciens Poëtes de la France, 4 (Paris, Bibliothèque Elzévirienne, 1860).

13.   *Gormont et Isembart*, ed. Alphonse Bayot, Classiques Français du Moyen Age, 14 (Paris, Champion, 3rd ed. 1931).

14.   Guillaume de Berneville, *La Vie de Saint Gilles*, ed. Gaston Paris and Alphonse Bos, Société des Anciens Textes Français (Paris, Firmin-Didot, 1881).

15.   *Historia Karoli Magni et Rotholandi ou Chronique du Pseudo-Turpin*, ed. C. Meredith Jones (Paris, 1936; repr. Geneva, Slatkine, 1972).

16.   *Huon de Bordeaux*, ed. Pierre Ruelle, Travaux de l'Université Libre de Bruxelles, Faculté de Philosophie et Lettres, 20 (Brussels, Presses Universitaires de Bruxelles, 1960).

17.   *La Chanson de Roland*, ed. and trans. Ian Short, Lettres Gothiques, 4524 (Paris, Librairie Générale Française, 1990).

18.   *La Chevalerie Vivien*, ed. Duncan McMillan, 2 vols, Senefiance, 39–40 (Aix-en-Provence, CUER MA, 1997).

19.   *La Poésie lyrique d'oïl, les origines et les premiers trouvères, textes d'études*, ed. I.M. Cluzel and L. Pressouyre (Paris, Nizet, 2nd ed. 1969).

20.   *Le Charroi de Nîmes, chanson de geste du XIIe siècle éditée d'après la rédaction AB*, ed. Duncan McMillan, Bibliothèque Française et Romane, B12 (Paris, Klincksieck, 2nd ed., 1978).

21.   *Les Deux Rédactions en vers du Moniage Guillaume*, ed. Wilhelm Cloetta, 2 Vols, Société des Anciens Textes Français (Paris, Firmin-Didot, 1906–11).

22.   *Les Enfances Guillaume, chanson de geste du XIIIe siècle*, ed. Patrice Henry, Société des Anciens Textes Français (Paris, SATF, 1935).

23.   *Les Lais de Marie de France*, ed. Jean Rychner, Classiques Français du Moyen Age, 93 (Paris, Champion, 1978).

24.   *Les Rédactions en vers du Couronnement de Louis*, ed. Yvan G. Lepage, Textes Littéraires Français, 261 (Geneva, Droz, 1978).

25.   *Les Romans de Chrétien de Troyes, I, Erec et Enide*, ed. Mario Roques, Classiques Français du Moyen Age, 80 (Paris, Champion, 1970).

26.   *Les Romans de Chrétien de Troyes, III, Le Chevalier de la Charrete*, ed. Mario Roques, Classiques Français du Moyen Age, 86 (Paris, Champion, 1958).

27.   *Les Romans de Chrétien de Troyes, IV, Le Chevalier au Lion (Yvain)*, ed. Mario Roques, Classiques Français du Moyen Age, 89 (Paris, Champion, 1965).

28. *Les Romans de Chrétien de Troyes, V, Le Conte du Graal (Perceval)*, ed. Félix Lecoy, 2 Vols, Classiques Français du Moyen Age, 100, 103 (Paris, Champion, 1984–90).

29. *Maugis d'Aigremont, chanson de geste*, ed. Philippe Vernay, Romanica Helvetica, 93 (Berne, Francke, 1980).

30. *Nouvelle anthologie de la lyrique occitane du moyen âge*, ed. Pierre Bec, Les Classiques d'Oc (Avignon, Aubanel, 1970).

31. *Piramus et Tisbé*, ed. C. De Boer, Classiques Français du Moyen Age, 26 (Paris, Champion, 1921).

32. *Raoul de Cambrai*, ed. Sarah Kay (Oxford, Clarendon Press, 1992).

33. Saint Bernard de Clairvaux, *Eloge de la nouvelle chevalerie*, ed. and trans. Pierre-Yves Emery (Paris, Editions du Cerf, 1990).

34. ——, *Textes politiques*, trans. P. Zumthor, Bibliothèque Médiévale, 10/18 (Paris, Union Générale d'Editions, 1986).

35. Tacitus, *The Agricola and the Germania*, trans. H. Mattingly, revised S.A. Handford, The Penguin Classics (Harmondsworth, Penguin Books, 1970).

36. *The Battle of Maldon and Other Old English Poems*, ed. B. Mitchell, trans. K. Crossley-Holland (London, Macmillan, 1965).

37. *The Song of Roland, an analytical edition*, ed. Gerard J. Brault, 2 Vols (University Park, Pennsylvania State University Press, 1978).

38. Vita de sancti Willelmo Duce postea Monacho Gellonense in Gallia, in Acta Sanctorum quotquot toto orbe coluntur...Maii, 8 Vols, ed. Joanne Carnadet, editio novissima (Paris, Victorem Palme, 1866).

STUDIES

39. Adler, Alfred, 'Guillaume, Vivien et Rainoart. Le souillé et le pur', *Romania*, 90 (1969), 1–13.

40. Andrieux-Reix, Nelly, '*Grant fu l'estor, grant fu la joie*: formes et formules de la fête épique — le cas d'*Aliscans*', in *Mourir aux Aliscans, Aliscans et la légende de Guillaume d'Orange*, ed. Jean Dufournet, Collection Unichamp (Paris, Champion, 1993), pp.9–30.

41. Auerbach, Erich, *Mimesis: the representation of reality in Western literature*, trans. Willard R. Trask (Princeton, Princeton University Press, 1969).

42. Bachelard, Gaston, *La Psychanalyse du feu*, NRF Idées (Paris, Gallimard, 1971).

43. Bakhtin, M., *L'Œuvre de François Rabelais et la culture populaire au Moyen Age et sous la Renaissance*, trans. A. Robel, Bibliothèque des Idées (Paris, Gallimard, 1970).

44. Baumgartner, Emmanuèle, '"Compiler/Acomplir"', in *Nouvelles recherches sur le Tristan en Prose*, ed. Jean Dufournet, Collection Unichamp (Paris, Champion, 1990).
45. Becker, Philipp August, *Der Liederkreis um Vivien*, Sitzungsberichte der Akademie der Wissenschaften in Wien, Philosophisch-historische Klasse, 223,1 (Vienna, Rudolph M. Rohrer, 1944).
46. Beckmann, Gustav Adolf, 'Das Beispiel Renewart: Geschichte und Folklore als Inspirationsquelle der altfranzösischen Epik', *Romanistisches Jahrbuch*, 22 (1971), 53–83.
47. Bédier, Joseph, *Les Légendes épiques, recherches sur la formation des chansons de geste*, 4 Vols (Paris, Champion, 1908–13).
48. Bennett, Philip E., 'Further Reflections on the Luminosity of the *Chanson de Roland*', *Olifant*, 4,3 (1977), 191–204.
49. ——, 'Havelok and Rainoart', *Folklore*, 90 (1979), 77–90.
50. ——, 'Le personnage de Huguelin dans *Gormont et Isembart*', *Marche Romane*, 29 (1979), 25–36.
51. ——, 'Guillaume d'Orange: Fighter of Demons and Harrower of Hell', in *Myth and Legend in French Literature, essays in honour of A.J. Steele*, ed. K. Aspley, D. Bellos and P. Sharratt (London, Modern Humanities Research Association, 1982), pp.24–46.
52. ——, 'The Storming of the Other World, the Enamoured Muslim Princess and the Evolution of the Legend of Guillaume d'Orange', in *Guillaume d'Orange and the Chanson de Geste, essays presented to Duncan McMillan in celebration of his seventieth birthday*, ed. Wolfgang van Emden and Philip E. Bennett (Reading, Société Rencesvals British Branch, 1984), pp.1–14.
53. ——, 'Le Pèlerinage de Charlemagne: le sens de l'aventure', in *Essor et fortune de la chanson de geste dans l'Europe et l'Orient latin, actes du IXe congrès international de la Société Rencesvals* (Modena, Mucchi, 1984), pp.475–87.
54. ——, '*La Chanson de Guillaume*, poème anglo-normand?', in *Au carrefour des routes d'Europe: la chanson de geste*, 2 Vols, Senefiance 20–21 (Aix-en-Provence, Publications du CUER MA, 1987), pp.259–81.
55. ——, 'L'épique dans l'historiographie anglo-normande: Gaimar, Wace, Jordan Fantosme', in *Aspects de l'épopée romane: mentalité, idéologies, intertextualités*, ed. Hans van Dijk and Willem Noomen, (Groningen, Forsten, 1995), pp.321–30.
56. Bergson, Henri, *Le Rire, essai sur la signification du comique* (Paris, Alcan, 13th ed., 1914).
57. Boutet, Dominique, '*Aliscans* et la problématique du héros épique médiéval', in *Comprendre et aimer la chanson de geste (à propos*

d'Aliscans), ed. Michèle Gally, Feuillets de l'ENS Fontenay-St Cloud (Fontenay aux Roses, ENS, 1994), pp.47–62.

58. Calin William, *The Epic Quest, studies in four Old French chansons de geste* (Baltimore, MA, The Johns Hopkins Press, 1966).

59. Campbell, Kimberlee Anne, 'Fighting Back: a survey of patterns of female aggressiveness in the Old French *chanson de geste*', in *Charlemagne in the North, proceedings of the twelfth international conference of the Société Rencesvals,* ed. Philip E. Bennett, Anne Elizabeth Cobby and Graham A. Runnalls (Edinburgh, Société Rencesvals British Branch, 1993), pp.241–51.

60. Carney, Anna P., 'A Portrait of the Hero as a Child: Guillaume, Roland, Girard and Gui', *Olifant,* 18, 3–4 (1993–94), 238–77.

61. Cerquiglini, Bernard, *Eloge de la variante, histoire critique de la philologie,* Des Travaux (Paris, Seuil, 1989).

62. Cobby, Anne Elizabeth, *Ambivalent Conventions: formula and parody in Old French,* Faux Titre, 101 (Amsterdam, Rodopi, 1995).

63. Colby-Hall, Alice, 'Le substrat arlésien de la *Prise d'Orange*', in *VIII Congreso de la Société Rencesvals* (Pamplona, Institución Principe de Viana, 1981), pp.83–86.

64. Combarieu du Grès, Micheline de, 'Les "nouveaux" chrétiens: Guibourc et Rainouart dans *Aliscans*', in *Mourir aux Aliscans* [see *40*], pp.55–77.

65. Crist, Larry S., 'Remarques sur la structure de la chanson de geste *Charroi de Nîmes-Prise d'Orange*' in *Charlemagne et l'épopée romane, Actes du VIIe Congrès International de la Société Rencesvals,* 2 Vols, Les Congrès et Colloques de l'Université de Liège, 76 (Liège, Université de Liège; Paris, 'Les Belles Lettres', 1978), pp.359–72.

66. Curtius, Ernst Robert, *European Literature and the Latin Middle Ages,* trans. Willard R. Trask, Bollingen Series, 36 (Princeton, Princeton University Press, 1952, repr. 1990).

67. De Caluwé, Jacques, 'La prière épique dans les plus anciennes chansons de geste', in *Hommage des romanistes liégeois à J. Wathelet-Willem, Marche Romane,* 26 (1976), 97–116.

68. Delbouille, Maurice, 'Les chansons de geste et le livre', in *La Technique littéraire des chansons de geste, actes du colloque de Liège (septembre 1957),* Bibliothèque de la Faculté de Philosophie et Lettres de l'Université de Liège, 150 (Paris, 'Les Belles Lettres', 1959), pp.295–407.

69. Dragonetti, Roger, *La Technique poétique des trouvères dans la chanson courtoise* (Bruges, De Tempel, 1960).

70. Duggan, Joseph J., *The Song of Roland: formulaic style and poetic craft,* Publications of the Center for Medieval and Renaissance

Studies, University of California, Los Angeles, 6 (Berkeley; Los Angeles, University of California Press, 1973).

71. Dumézil, Georges, *Mythes et épopées I. II. III*, Quarto (Paris, Gallimard, 1995, original editions 1968–73).

72. Frappier, Jean, *Les Chansons de geste du cycle de Guillaume d'Orange*, 2 Vols (Paris, SEDES, 1955–67).

73. Genette, Gérard, *Palimpsestes: la littérature au second degré*, Collection Poétique (Paris, Seuil, 1982).

74. Grégoire, Henri, 'Comment Guillaume de Toulouse devint Guillaume d'Orange', *Provence Historique*, 1 (1950–51), 32–44.

75. Grisward, Joël-Henri, *Archéologie de l'épopée médiévale: structures trifonctionnelles et mythes indo-européens dans le cycle des Narbonnais*, Bibliothèque Historique (Paris, Payot, 1981).

76. Grunmann-Gaudet, Minnette, 'From Epic to Romance: the paralysis of the hero in the *Prise d'Orange*', *Olifant*, 7,1 (1979), 22–38.

77. Guidot, Bernard, '*Aliscans*: structures parentales ou filiations spirituelles?', in *Les Relations de parenté dans le monde médiéval*, Senefiance, 26 (Aix-en-Provence, Publications du CUER MA, 1989), pp.25–45.

78. Györy, Jean, 'Epaves archaïques dans *Gormont et Isembart*', in *Mélanges offerts à René Crozet*, Supplément aux *Cahiers de Civilisation Médiévale* (Poitiers, Société d'Etudes Médiévales, 1966), pp.675–84.

79. Harvey, John, *Mediæval Gardens* (London, Batsford, 1981).

80. Heinemann, Edward A., *L'Art métrique de la chanson de geste, essai sur la musicalité du récit*, Publications Romanes et Françaises, 205 (Geneva, Droz, 1993).

81. Hitze, Renate, *Studien zu Sprache und Stil der Kampfschilderungen in den Chansons de Geste*, Kölner Romanistische Arbeiten, neue Folge, 33 (Geneva, Droz, 1965).

82. Hoggan, David G., 'La formation du noyau cyclique: *Couronnement de Louis-Charroi de Nîmes-Prise d'Orange*', in *Société Rencesvals, Proceedings of the Fifth Conference (Oxford, 1970)*, ed. G. R. Mellor (Salford, University of Salford, 1977), pp.22–44.

83. Hunt, Tony, 'La parodie médiévale: le cas d'*Aucassin et Nicolette*', *Romania*, 100 (1979), 341–81.

84. Jackson, W.T.H., *The Hero and the King: an epic theme* (New York, Columbia University Press, 1982).

85. Kay, Sarah, 'The Character of Character in the *Chansons de Geste*', in *The Craft of Fiction, essays in medieval poetics*, ed. Leigh A. Arrathoon (Rochester MI, Solaris Press, 1984), pp.475–98.

86. Koss, Ronald G., *Family, Kinship and Lineage in the* Cycle de Guillaume d'Orange, Studies in Medieval Literature, 5 (Lewiston; Queenstown; Lampeter, Edwin Mellen, 1990).

87. Kullmann, Dorothea, *Verwandtschaft in epischer Dichtung, Untersuchungen zu den französischen 'chansons de geste' des 12. Jahrhunderts*, Beiheft zur *Zeitschrift für romanische Philologie*, 242 (Tübingen, Niemeyer, 1992).

88. Labbé, Alain, *L'Architecture des palais et des jardins dans les chansons de geste: essai sur le thème du roi en majesté* (Paris, Champion; Geneva, Slatkine, 1987).

89. ——, 'De la cuisine à la salle: topographie d'*Aliscans* et l'évolution du personnage de Rainouart', in *Mourir aux Aliscans* [see *40*], pp.209–26.

90. Lachet, Claude, *La Prise d'Orange ou la parodie courtoise d'une épopée*, Nouvelle Bibliothèque du Moyen Age, 10 (Paris, Champion, 1986).

91. Lawrence, C.H., *Medieval Monasticism: forms of religious life in Western Europe in the Middle Ages* (London, Longman, 1984).

92. Le Gentil, Pierre, *La Chanson de Roland*, Connaissance des Lettres (Paris, Hatier, 1967).

93. Lehmann, Paul, *Die Parodie im Mittelalter* (München, Drei Masken Verlag, 1922).

94. Lonigan, P., 'Lyricism and Narration in the *Gormont et Isembart* Fragment', *Neophilologus*, 54 (1970), 31–8.

95. Lord, A.B., *The Singer of Tales*, Harvard Studies in Comparative Literature, 24 (Cambridge, Mass., Harvard University Press, 1960).

96. MacInnes, John W., 'Gloriette: the function of the tower and the name in the *Prise d'Orange*', *Olifant*, 10, 1–2 (1982–83), 24–40.

97. Martin, Jean-Pierre, '"Vue de la fenêtre" ou "panorama épique": structures rhétoriques et fonctions narratives', in *Au carrefour des routes d'Europe* [see *54*], pp.859–78.

98. ——, *Les Motifs dans la chanson de geste: définition et utilisation*, Discours de l'épopée médiévale, 1 (Lille, Centre d'études médiévales et dialectales de l'Université de Lille III, 1992).

99. ——, 'Le personnage de Rainouart, entre épopée et carnaval', in *Comprendre et aimer la chanson de geste* [see *57*], pp.63–86.

100. McMillan, Duncan, 'Orable fille de Desramé' in *Mélanges offerts à Rita Lejeune*, 2 Vols (Gembloux, Duculot, 1969), 2, pp.829–54.

101. ——, '*La Prise d'Orange* dans le manuscrit français 1448' in *Actes du VIe Congrès International de la Société Rencesvals* (Aix-en-Provence, Université de Provence, 1974), pp.541–60.

132   *La Chanson de Guillaume* and *La Prise d'Orange*

102. Ménard, Philippe, *Le Rire et le sourire dans le roman courtois en France au moyen âge (1150–1250)*, Publications Romanes et Françaises, 105 (Geneva, Droz, 1969).

103. Menéndez-Pidal, Ramón, *La Chanson de Roland et la tradition épique des Francs*, revised R. Louis, trans. I.-R. Cluzel (Paris, Picard, 1960).

104. Myers-Ivey, Sharon, 'Repetitive Patterns for Introducing Speech in the Manuscript Tradition of the *Prise d'Orange*', *Olifant*, 8,1 (1980), 51–65.

105. ——, 'A Thematic and Formulaic Study of the Manuscript Tradition of *La Prise d'Orange*' (PhD, University of California, Berkeley, 1982; University Microfilms International, 1985).

106. Neuschäfer, Hans-Jörg, '*Le Voyage de Charlemagne* als Parodie der chanson de geste: Untersuchungen zur Epenparodie im Mittelalter (1)', *Romanistisches Jahrbuch*, 10 (1959), 78–102.

107. Nykrog, Per, *Les Fabliaux*, Publications Romanes et Françaises, 123 (Geneva, Droz, 1973).

108. Pastré, Jean-Marc, 'Rainoart et Rennewart: un guerrier aux cuisines' in *Burlesque et dérision dans les épopées de l'Occident médiéval*, ed. B. Guidot, Annales Littéraires de l'Université de Besançon, 558, Série Littéraire, 3 (Besançon, Presses de l'Université, 1995), pp.123–31.

109. Pickens, Rupert T., 'Art épique et verticalisation: problèmes narratifs dans le *Couronnement de Louis*', *Vox Romanica*, 45 (1986), 116–49.

110. Press, Alan, '"S'en a un ris gité" in the *Charroi de Nîmes*', *Forum for Modern Language Studies*, 12 (1976), 17–24.

111. ——, '"S'en a un ris gité" in the *Charroi de Nîmes*: a further note', *Forum for Modern Language Studies*, 14 (1978), 42–46.

112. Propp, Vladimir, *Morphology of the Folktale* (Austin, University of Texas Press, 1968).

113. Régnier, Claude, 'La *Prise d'Orange* dans le manuscrit B.N. fr. 1448', *Travaux de Linguistique et de Littérature*,16 (1978), 439–47.

114. Robertson, Howard S., *La Chanson de Willame, a critical study*, University of North Carolina Studies in the Romance Languages and Literatures, 65 (Chapel Hill, University of North Carolina Press, 1966).

115. Rychner, Jean, *La Chanson de geste, essai sur l'art épique des jongleurs*, Publications Romanes et Françaises, 53 (Geneva, Droz, 1955).

116. Southern, R.W., *The Making of the Middle Ages*, Hutchinson University Library (London, Hutchinson, 1967).

117. Suard, François, 'Le motif du déguisement dans quelques chansons du cycle de Guillaume d'Orange', *Olifant*, 7,4 (1980), 343–58.

118. The Princeton Encyclopedia of Poetry and Poetics, ed. Alex Preminger, Frank J. Warnke and O.B. Hardison Jr (Princeton, Princeton University Press, enlarged ed. 1974).

119. The Year 1200: a symposium, ed. François Avril (New York, Metropolitan Museum of Art, 1975).

120. Thompson, Stith, *Motif-Index of Folk-Literature : a classification of narrative elements in folktales, ballads, myths, fables, mediaeval romances, exempla, fabliaux, jest-books and local legends*, Rev. ed., 6 Vols (Copenhagen, Rosenkilde and Bagger, 1955–58).

121. Trotter, D.A., *Medieval French Literature and the Crusades (1100–1300)*, Histoire des Idées et Critique Littéraire, 256 (Geneva, Droz, 1988).

122. Van Emden, Wolfgang G., '"E cil de France le cleiment a guarant": Roland, Vivien et le thème du "guarant"', in *Rencesvals VI* [see *101*], pp.31–61.

123. ——, '*Girart de Vienne* devant les ordinateurs', in *La Chanson de geste et le mythe carolingien, mélanges René Louis*, ed. A. Moisan, 2 Vols (Saint-Père-sous-Vézelay, Musée Archéologique Régional, 1982), 2, pp.663–90.

124. Wailes, Stephen, 'The *Niebelungenlied* as Heroic Epic', in *Heroic Epic and Saga: an introduction to the world's great folk epics*, ed. F. Oinas and R.M. Dorson (Bloomington, Indiana University Press, 1978), pp.120–43.

125. Walter, Philippe, 'Rainouart et le marteau-tonneau: essai de mythologie épique et pantagruélique', *L'Information Littéraire*, 46 (1994), 3–14.

126. Warren, F.M., 'The Enamored Moslem Princess in Orderic Vital and the Old French Epic', *Publications of the Modern Language Association*, 29 (1914), 341–58.

127. Wathelet-Willem, Jeanne, 'Charlemagne et Guillaume', in *Charlemagne et l'épopée romane* [see *65*], pp.215–22.

128. ——, 'Guillaume, mari ridicule et complaisant?', in *Mélanges d'histoire littéraire, de linguistique et de philologie romane offerts à Charles Rostaing par ses collègues, ses élèves et ses amis*, 2 Vols (Liège, Association des Romanistes de Liège, 1974), pp.1213–33.

129. ——, 'Quelle est l'origine du tinel de Rainouart?', *Boletin de la Real Academia de Buenas Letras de Barcelona*, 31 (1965–66), 355–64.

130. ——, 'Rainouart et son cycle', *Mittelalterstudien. Erich Köhler zum Gedenken*, ed. Henning Krauss and Dietmar Rieger, Studia Romanica, 55 (Heidelberg, Carl Winter Verlag, 1984), pp.288–300.

131. ——, *Recherches sur la Chanson de Guillaume, études accompagnées d'une édition*, 2 Vols, Bibl. de la Faculté de Philosophie et Lettres de l'Université de Liège, 210 (Paris, 'Les Belles Lettres', 1975).

132. Wilmotte, Maurice, 'La Chanson de Roland et la Chanson de Willame', *Romania*, 44 (1915–17), 53–86.

133. Wilson, Colin, *The Outsider* (London, Gollancz, 1956).

134. *World Architecture, an illustrated history*, ed. Trewin Copplestone (London, Paul Hamlyn, 1963).

135. Zumthor, Paul, 'Les *planctus* épiques', *Romania*, 84 (1963), 61–69.

136. ——, *Essai de poétique médiévale*, Coll. Poétique (Paris, Seuil, 1972).